LED ZEPPELIN

PETER GRANT in association with NANDA and RON LESLEY
★ PROUDLY PRESENT AT BLUESVILLE ★

BATHS HALL - IPSWICH
TUESDAY, NOV. 16
FOR ONE APPEARANCE ONLY
★ ★ ★ ★ ★ ★ ★ ★ ★ ★ ★

INTERNATIONALLY FAMOUS
LED ZEPPELIN
★ ★ ★ ★ ★ ★ ★ ★ ★ ★ ★

TICKETS £1 EACH ON SALE DAILY
AT BATHS HALL BOX OFFICE, IPSWICH (TEL. IPSWICH 53882)
AND ON NIGHT PERFORMANCE 8 — 11 P.M.

THIS IS A CARLTON BOOK

Published in Great Britain in 2015 by
Carlton Books Limited
20 Mortimer Street
London W1T 3JW

Previously published as *Treasures of Led Zeppelin* in 2010.

Copyright 2015 © Carlton Books Limited

A CIP catalogue for this book is available from
the British Library.

ISBN 978-1-78097-648-8

Printed in China

10 9 8 7 6 5 4 3 2 1

LED ZEPPELIN

CHRIS WELCH

CARLTON
BOOKS

CONTENTS

PREVIOUS PAGE: The handbill for a concert at St Matthew's Baths Hall in Ipswich, UK from 1971.

LEFT: The biggest band in the world, pictured here at their peak in 1973, gave the world the definitive template for rock and roll.

OVERLEAF: The song may have remained the same, but the world changed, post-Zeppelin, pictured here in 1973.

THE EARLY YEARS

The treasures sought by Jimmy Page were artists whose skills and charisma would "glister like gold" in the eyes of the beholders. More practically, he wanted the best musicians available to fulfil his dream of creating the ultimate supergroup.

Formed in 1962, The Yardbirds had made their name on the British R&B scene, having taken over the residency at Richmond's noted Crawdaddy club, that had recently been vacated by The Rolling Stones. They had their own high-energy take on the Chicago electric blues of such celebrated players as Howlin' Wolf and Muddy Waters. They also had their own trump card in the form of a young blues-obsessed guitarist named Eric Clapton, who quickly established himself as the leading player on the British scene. The Yardbirds enjoyed plenty of critical acclaim, but when manager Giorgio Gomelsky took them into the studio to create a more commercial sound an unexpected run of chart hits ensued, among them 'For Your Love' and 'Good Morning Little Schoolgirl'.

With success, however, came problems – the main one being Clapton's objection to the band's new pop direction. Shortly afterwards he left to join up with the "purist" idealogy of John Mayall's Bluesbreakers. Before departing, Clapton recommended taking a look at Jimmy Page, who in spite of his youth was already a well-respected session player. But already making a very good livelihood from his work, Page decided not to risk it for the uncertainty of life in a pop group with all that touring. He recommended his friend Jeff Beck.

With Beck in position, The Yardbirds emerged with a much tougher R&B sound, the guitarist's influential fuzz and distortion sound at the very centre of such classic hits as 'Heart Full of Soul' and 'I'm A Man'. When, in 1966, bass player Paul Samwell-Smith decided to retire, the band's second guitarist, Chris Dreja, agreed to take over on bass. While he was learning, Jimmy Page took on bass playing responsibilities. When Dreja was up to speed, Page stayed on board, and The Yardbirds now featured the mouth-watering proposition of a twin-lead line-up featuring two of what were at the time Britain's hottest young players.

The new line-up turned out to be very short-lived, and recorded very little new music. In October 1966, whilst on tour in the US during a stop-off in Texas, Beck was fired from the group. During the year that followed, The Yardbirds found their popularity on the wane, and by the end of 1967, whilst still popular on the US live circuit, the hits had all but dried up.

The idea of creating a band like Led Zeppelin had remained with Jimmy Page since 1966. Whilst still a Yardbird, Jeff Beck went into the studio to record a track entitled 'Beck's Bolero' – a rock instrumental based around Maurice Ravel's famed 20th-century classical piece, 'Bolero'. The line-up assembled in the studio comprised Beck and Page on guitar, Nicky Hopkins

BELOW: Yet to meet, Jimmy Page and John Paul Jones were both successful session musicians, Robert Plant was in the Birmingham band Hobbstweedle and with John Bonham in Band of Joy.

OPPOSITE: Assorted Yardbirds memorabilia. Their headline at the Fillmore Auditorium in New York is testament to the band's success in the US.

of the Rolling Stones on piano, session bass player and arranger John Paul Jones, and The Who's Keith Moon on drums. The track is consired by many critics to be an early milestone in the development of both the heavy rock and progressive rock genres. It has also been the subject of much disagreement as to who actually wrote the track. Page is credited as the composer and producer but Beck maintains that it was largely *his* work. In 1977 Page would bluntly give his opinion on the matter when interviewed in the US magazine *Trouser Press*: "I wrote it, played on it, produced it … and I don't give a damn what he [Beck] says. That's the truth."

(Amusingly, given it's considered pre-eminence, the track would first come to light a year later when it appeared as the B-side of Beck's unlikely hit single 'Hi Ho Silver Lining'. In spite of only reaching Number 14 in the charts it has bafflingly remained a cheesy dance-floor hardy annual for every generation that has since followed.)

This intriguing band line-up had given Page the idea of forming a regular group with Beck, Moon and Hopkins, only with Moon's bandmate John Entwistle on bass. (Surprisingly, the drummer and bassist were contemplating quitting The Who at this time.) But if it was to get off the ground they needed a powerful young singer. Stevie Winwood and Steve Marriott were obvious choices of the time. Both, however, were otherwise engaged: Winwood was involved with Traffic and Marriot was signed to the Small Faces. Marriott's manager emphasised that he would not be

allowed to join this new project, as Page commented: "I got a call saying, 'How would you like to play guitar with broken fingers?'"

The idea was taken no further and Page concentrated on his efforts as the sole lead guitarist with The Yardbirds, introducing a slow hard-edged blues-rocker called 'Dazed And Confused', on which he would used a violin bow on the guitar strings for dramatic effect.

The Yardbirds continued to struggle on, but with forthright differing views within their ranks as to the direction they should take, it was a band on the edge of certain collapse.

Meanwhile, in the Midlands, a new group called Band of Joy was trying to establish itself. Featuring a blues singer named Robert Plant and a hard-hitting drummer named John Bonham, they had already established a local reputation for psychedelic light shows and a powerful live sound, but with no record deal in sight they were struggling to make ends meet.

BELOW: Band of Joy, featuring both Robert Plant (second from left) and John Bonham (centre).

SUNDAY JULY 3rd

NORTH PIER

AT **6** & **8** P.M.   BOOKABLE SEATS **7/6** & **9/6**

Telephone: 20900   Box Office open 10 a.m.

AUSTIN NEWMAN presents

The Fabulous

YARDBIRDS

"OVER-UNDER-SIDEWAYS-DOWN"

THOSE WILD THINGS

THE TROGGS

BLACKPOOL'S   COMPERE

THE **TRIANGLE** | JERRY STEVENS

LIVERPOOL'S No. 1

THE CARROLLS

Sun., 10th July—THE SPENCER DAVIS GROUP

Hastings Printing Company. Drury Lane. St. Leonards-on-Sea. Sussex. Telephone Hastings 2450

"HOW WOULD YOU LIKE TO PLAY GUITAR WITH BROKEN FINGERS?"

Steve Marriott's then-manager, the legendary Don Arden, to Jimmy Page, during the formation of Led Zeppelin.

LEFT: North Pier poster. 1966 saw the Yardbirds on an extensive touring circuit. Jimmy Page and Jeff Beck were part of the band at that point. This classic style poster was for a gig in Blackpool, UK.

RIGHT: Whole lotta hair. An early photo shoot see the band in serious, reflective poses, 1968.

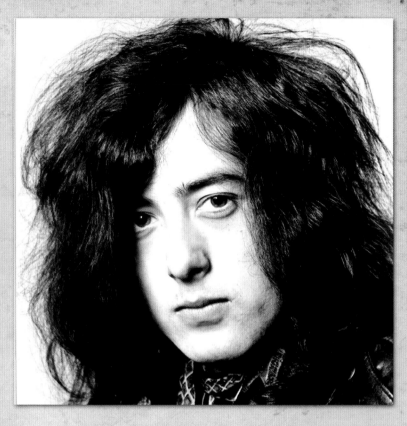

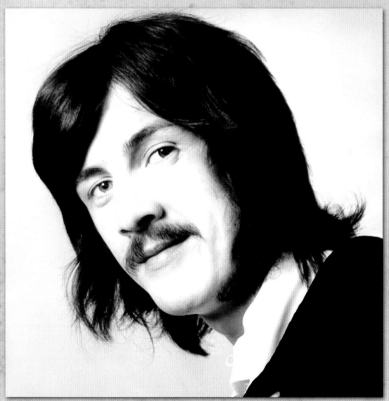

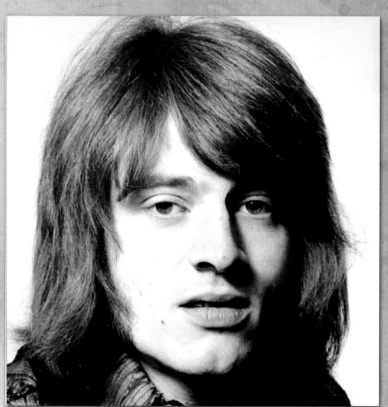

1968

Jimmy Page had already had his vision of a rock supergroup. But this was an era when a plethora of dynamic groups had already been established. How would it be possible to take on The Who, Cream and The Jimi Hendrix Experience? But Page, aged only 21, was well placed to try. His session background meant that he knew how studios worked and, having already toured North America with The Yardbirds, he could see the potential audience for ever more powerful rock bands.

During 1967 rifts had begun to grow within The Yardbirds. Original members Keith Relf and Jim McCarty wanted to pursue a style influenced by folk and classical music; Jimmy Page, at a time when the psychedelic blues-rock of Cream and The Jimi Hendrix Experience was massively popular, wanted to go for a "heavier" sound. By March 1968 Relf and McCarty had decided to leave, but were persuaded to stay on for one more US tour. As far as the music was concerned, Page began to get his own way, and during the tour the kind of new rock sound he had in mind gradually came to the fore. The Yardbirds returned to England in the summer of 1968. After one final appearance at Luton Technical College in July it was all over. The band split.

Page was keen to carry on, and, as The Yardbirds had a contracted tour in Scandinavia still outstanding, he invited rhythm guitarist-turned-bass player Chris Dreja to form part of the new outfit. But after six years on the road Dreja opted instead for a new life. He had recently become interested in photography and decided to try it professionally.

Jimmy Page, thinking back to his earlier notion of a "supergroup", set about creating a new band. He first approached

John Paul Jones, an arranger and organist as well as a bass player with whom he'd worked on Donovan's 'Hurdy Gurdy Man'. Page explained there were Yardbirds dates unfilled and he planned to call his replacement outfit "The New Yardbirds". Terry Reid, a solo singer signed to producer Mickie Most, was approached to front the band, but uninterested, he suggested a promising blues vocalist he'd spotted in the Midlands. 18-year-old Robert Plant had been with Band of Joy and had just begun fronting the curiously named Hobbstweedle. Page and Grant went to see him singing at a teachers training college gig in Birmingham and were immediately impressed; Page invited him to his home in Pangbourne, Berkshire, and they quickly realized they had very similar musical tastes. The group now had a vocalist, lead guitarist, bass player and keyboardist. All they needed now was a solid drummer.

Page had been thinking about asking B J Wilson, now playing with Procol Harum, but Plant suggested that he try out his old colleague from Band of Joy, one John Henry Bonham. At that time enjoying regular income backing visiting American singer Tim Rose, Plant persuaded "Bonzo" to come aboard with promises of fame and fortune. Even if Bonham didn't quite believe him, he liked the music that was on offer.

The group met in September in Soho for its first rehearsal. Page later commented: "The four of us got together in this room and started playing. Then we knew it would work and started laughing. Maybe it was from relief, or maybe from knowledge we could groove together. And that was it."

In October Jimmy Page visited the *Melody Maker* office in Fleet Street. The resulting interview was headlined "Only Jimmy Left To Form New Yardbirds." By the time it appeared "The New Yardbirds" had already played their first dates, fulfilling their tour obligations in Scandinavia.

It was clear now that the band could easily be accused of operating under false pretences since nobody in the band had any connection whatsoever with The Yardbirds' classic hits. They agreed a new name was needed. One account of what happened next is that Keith Moon and John Entwistle had previously remarked that a possible supergroup containing themselves, Jimmy Page and Jeff Beck would go down like a "lead zeppelin" – a term Entwistle used to describe a bad gig. The group were purported to have deliberately dropped the "a" from "Lead" at the suggestion of their manager, ex-wrestler and showbix tough guy, Peter Grant, to prevent "thick Americans" from pronouncing it "Leed". Page himself wasn't that bothered: "The name wasn't really as important as whether or not the music was going to be accepted… We could have called ourselves The Vegetables or The Potatoes, but I was quite keen on Led Zeppelin."

The group began recording a debut album at Olympic Studios in Barnes, London, while Grant set about booking gigs in the UK. They made their debut billed as "Led Zeppelin" at Surrey University on October 15, 1968. Three days later they played The Marquee in London to a good crowd. Larger venues followed, including Liverpool University on October 19 and the Roundhouse in London on November 11. After more university dates in Manchester and Sheffield they returned to the Marquee on December 10.

The British media, however, were still mostly ignoring the new band. Impatient with the UK's response, manager Peter Grant decided to take his "boys" to America. On Boxing Day 1968, Led Zeppelin made their American debut at Denver Coliseum, supporting Vanilla Fudge and The MC5.

They were an immediate hit. Staying on in the US, when they opened for another popular American rock group, Iron Butterfly, the headliners were so astounded by the reaction they refused to go on.

Led Zeppelin had arrived, and the rock world would never be the same again.

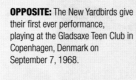

OPPOSITE: The New Yardbirds give their first ever performance, playing at the Gladsaxe Teen Club in Copenhagen, Denmark on September 7, 1968.

RIGHT: One of the first gigs with the band billed as "Led Zeppelin".

BELOW: (left to right) John Paul Jones, Jimmy Page, Robert Plant and John Bonham: about to change the course of rock music.

1969

America fell in love with Led Zeppelin in 1969. The debut album was released in January and New York columnist June Harris exclaimed: "Zeppelin is the new Cream!"

The decision to hit America was an easy one for Led Zeppelin, as Page explained: "I knew you could sit around as a new group for months in England and have no notice taken of you at all. In the States a group can get so much more exposure."

The first Led Zeppelin tour ended in February at Bill Graham's Fillmore East in New York, then a premier rock showcase. More important was the extensive radio play and promotion by Atlantic Records. Entering the *Billboard* Top 40 in February, the band's debut was in the Top Twenty by March.

Released in the UK on March 28, it received more rave reviews. "Jimmy Page Triumphs – Led Zeppelin is a gas!" exulted *Melody Maker*. The group flew home for more promotion, fitted in a swift trip to Scandinavia and popped up on BBC2's *How Late It Is* performing 'Communication Breakdown'.

That month they appeared in UK movie *Supershow*, a pioneering attempt at capturing rock and jazz acts on film. The sessions took place at a studio in Staines and also featured Eric Clapton, Stephen Stills, Buddy Miles, the Modern Jazz Quartet, Roland Kirk, Buddy Guy and Colosseum.

On April 24 the second US tour began, opening at the Fillmore West, San Francisco, alongside Brian Auger and Julie Driscoll. The first full UK tour started at Birmingham Town Hall on June 13, a Midlands homecoming for Plant and Bonham. At the Bath Festival on June 28, 12,000 fans flocked to see them. The following night they performed at London's Royal Albert Hall for the "Pop Proms", supported by Blodwyn Pig and Liverpool Scene.

Although they were expected to continue work on the album *Led Zeppelin II*, the call of America proved too strong and a third US tour began on July 5. More than 20 dates included jazz festivals in Newport, Baltimore and Philadelphia. They missed the Woodstock festival but, given the conditions, it was probably just as well, avoiding direct competition with Jimi Hendrix and Alvin Lee's Ten Years After. The third tour ended in August at the Texas International Pop Festival in Lewisville.

Page noted: "At most of the places we play we seem to get mass hysteria. In Boston all the boys in the front row were beating heads in time. When we started the group we only had enough material for 50 minutes but now this has extended to two hours. The American reaction is more than we ever dreamed could happen."

Some critics had not fully understood the "headbanging" heavy rock revolution Led Zeppelin was fomenting. Asked if they would turn down the volume, Page replied: "No – we're getting louder. Our drummer's amazingly loud. I come off stage with my ears singing."

By now the band was earning $30,000 a night. It was time for a holiday; Page went to Morocco, where he was exposed

ABOVE: The band was an immediate success as soon as they touched down in the USA.

to what became known as "world music". Back in Britain the band finished off *Led Zeppelin II* at Olympic Studios and played a triumphant concert at the Lyceum Ballroom in the Strand on October 12 – the 54th anniversary of a real Zeppelin raid, when the Lyceum was bombed. When a relative of Count Zeppelin complained about the use of the name by a group of "shrieking monkeys", Jimmy briefly considered renaming the band The Nobs to placate her, but by now "Led Zeppelin" was as famous as any airship.

Days later it was back to New York for two concerts at Carnegie Hall – one of the first rock concerts at the venue that was much better known for classical and jazz events. It was especially important for Bonham, as his idols Gene Krupa and Buddy Rich had played on the same stage. Young New Yorkers' exuberance was in contrast to the more reserved attitude among British fans. There was also none of the cynicism they encountered at home. As Plant observed: "A lot of people in Britain have been against us for some reason … they say we're a made-up manufactured group because we were successful right away, but we just got together in the same way all groups get together. We had to prove ourselves on stage. From then on it just grew."

By October all the focus was on the release of *Led Zeppelin II*. At Atlantic's Manhattan offices the staff excitedly blew up rubber Led Zeppelin balloons and shouted to anyone who would listen: "Led Zeppelin and The Who are the two biggest acts in America. It's like The Monkees never existed!"

The album was released on October 22 in America and had advance orders of 400,000. Within a couple of weeks it was Number 2. The stand-out track, 'Whole Lotta Love', would become not only the band's anthem but the signature tune for BBC TV's *Top of the Pops*. Ironically, the band refused to allow it to be put out as a single in the UK, although an edited version was sent to US radio stations; a single version shot to Number 4 in the *Billboard* chart by December. Grant was still against releasing singles, despite Atlantic's demands; if anybody wanted a particular song, they'd have to buy the album. Zeppelin didn't want to be regarded as a "pop singles" band. They were certainly taken seriously by the UK government, as they were high earners and tax-payers. On December 11, at London's Savoy Hotel. Gwyneth Dunwoody, Parliamentary Secretary to the Board of Trade, presented them with one gold and two platinum albums in recognition of their American sales.

When Page turned up to buy a brand-new Rolls-Royce at a showroom in Berkeley Square his long hair and flamboyant clothes might have startled the salesmen but they soon realized he meant business, as did Bonham when he walked into a Birmingham showroom with £10,000 and bought a Maserati. The new rock royalty had arrived.

RIGHT: The legendary Fillmore East venue, New York, takes a beating, May 1 1969.

BELOW: Robert Plant and Maureen Wilson were married on November 9 1968.

RIGHT: A wild guitar-swinging axe-hero on stage, Jimmy was often quiet and contemplative off it.

OVERLEAF: Zeppelin shake the Fillmore East hall to the rafters, New York, May 1 1969.

LED ZEPPELIN

When early review copies of *Led Zeppelin* arrived at music magazines and radio stations from London to New York, they were seized upon with the same eager expectation albums by The Beatles were accorded in previous years.

The media buzz was matched by fans' growing fervour as word spread about the impending assault. They were not disappointed. When the arms of record players began descending on to the black vinyl for the first time, pounding guitar riffs from Page and screaming vocals from Plant signalled the birth of a new era.

The album had been recorded at Olympic Studios during a nine-day period in October 1968. Engineer Glyn Johns recalled the band spent only 30 hours in the studio at a cost of £1,782. However, between band and producer they managed to capture the essence of their rapidly evolving style.

Led Zeppelin had only been together two and a half weeks when they began recording, but at least they had worked out and practised the material at rehearsals and gigs. An urgency and excitement permeated the nine tracks that would make history and assure the future of the band.

They also had very clear aims and, unlike many young musicians, were not intimidated by the studio environment. Said Page: "We were deliberately aiming at putting down what we could already reproduce on stage. I wanted to use a lot of contrast and get an ambient sound, and I wanted light and shade and dramatic tension."

The penetrating, often eerie sound was partly the result of using backwards tape echo. This complemented the mood and progression of songs that seemed to grow organically. Each track had its own life and identity and was akin to classical "programme music" in structure.

The opening salvo, 'Good Times Bad Times', quickly established the stylistic strands that set Zeppelin apart. Whereas the average rock outfit would charge through a 12-bar blues with little thought for dynamics, Zeppelin utilized interplay between vocals and guitar, interspersed solos with breaks and sometimes stopped altogether, allowing a pregnant silence to create additional tension.

"In the days of my youth I was told what it was to be a man!" was Plant's opening statement, matched by an ongoing commentary from Bonham, Page and Jones whose improvisational skills were born out of jazz and blues.

'Babe I'm Gonna Leave You', a song by Anne Bredon found on a Joan Baez album, had intrigued Page since his session days; it was one of the tunes he suggested they might cover at initial meetings with Plant. The Zeppelin version evolves into a clever arrangement full of twists and turns, lulls and crescendos with both electric and acoustic guitars brought into play.

'You Shook Me', a Willie Dixon tune previously recorded by Muddy Waters, also featured on Jeff Beck's 1968 album *Truth*. A thunderous blues, with fine harmonica-playing from Plant, it featured a spine-tingling guitar and vocal glissando. John Paul Jones' organ underpins the piece, climaxed by a sensational guitar break from Page.

'Dazed And Confused' creeps up on listeners with its ominous walking bass line. As an arrangement, it turns into a remarkable tour de force for the group. Jimmy also reintroduces his spectacular use of a violin bow on his guitar, first suggested by actor David McCallum's father, a professional violinist impressed by the young Page's playing during a recording session. Page thought it might be difficult but it produced spectacular results. He would use the bow with The Yardbirds and his later band The Firm, but its deployment on tunes such as 'How Many More Times', 'Good Times Bad Times' and 'Dazed And Confused' made it synonymous with Zeppelin.

'Your Time Is Gonna Come' is launched with Jones' church organ providing an ethereal sound before Robert launches into his protest about a girl who goes "Lying, cheating, hurting… that's all you ever seem to do…" Jimmy uses a Fender pedal steel guitar also employed on 'Babe I'm Gonna Leave You'.

Even more atmospheric is 'Black Mountain Side' a two-minute guitar instrumental that fades in during the closing seconds of the previous track. Page's repeated riff is complemented by tabla from Indian musician Viram Jasani. This hypnotic piece has its roots in Bert Jansch's 'Black Water Side' and the Page composition was often performed during the quieter acoustic medley squeezed into a live show.

In complete contrast comes the joyful explosion of 'Communication Breakdown'. The image of a bare-chested Plant strutting the stage and screaming "Communication breakdown, baby!" came to symbolize Zeppelin in full-on rock 'n' roll mode. Played at breakneck speed, it became the band's anthem, until supplanted by 'Whole Lotta Love' from their next album. Recalls Page: "The idea of 'Communication Breakdown' was to have a really raw, hard-hitting number. It was so exciting and electrifying and always so good to play, so staccato and a knock-out to do."

Taking a deep breath, the band dropped into a slower tempo for 'I Can't Quit You Baby' which became a favourite among all serious fans and those who most appreciated their grasp of the blues. Page's almost neurotic, desultory guitar notes soon give way to a beautifully constructed solo. A Willie Dixon song previously recorded by Otis Rush, it was another highlight.

'How Many More Times' has more walking bass that urges the group into a series of experimental passages which are more psychedelia than R&B. It includes a trademark exchange of ideas between Bonham and Page before Plant exclaims, "Oh Rosie, steal away now" over a marching rhythm.

This combination of fresh ideas and vibrant performances left most listeners stunned. Reviews of the record were

mostly positive, although it still took a while for the media to catch up. While the band went on a tour of the UK album sales began to mount and by April 1969 *Led Zeppelin* was in the Top Ten, entering at Number 6, and would stay there for 22 weeks. It was already a Top Ten hit in America and soon went gold.

JOHN PAUL JONES

The quiet man of the group, John Paul Jones brought a classical grandeur and elegance to their work. Although Plant and Bonham were "new boys" when they joined, "JPJ" knew Jimmy Page well before its formation, having played with him on many sessions.

BELOW: Zeppelin's own Renaissance Man – John Paul Jones could play bass, guitar and the keyboard. And he was no slouch when it came to composing string arrangements.

He was born John Baldwin in Sidcup, Kent, on January 3, 1946. Father Joe, a pianist and arranger, had worked with many top British dance bands, and had taught himself piano from the age of six. "I was a choirmaster and organist at our local church at the age of 14," he recalled. "That was how I earned the money to pay for my first bass guitar."

John went to boarding school in Blackheath aged five, because his parents were travelling the world in a musical variety act. He then spent three years at Eltham Green comprehensive school, but didn't do too well in his exams, "mainly because I was out playing in bands at American Air Force bases."

As a teenager John quickly absorbed a wide range of popular music influences. He loved the blues of Big Bill Broonzy as much as Rachmaninoff and was soon immersed in the soul and R&B hits of the Sixties. One of the tracks that inspired him to take up bass guitar was 'You Can't Sit Down' by the Phil Upchurch Combo.

His first regular group, at 15, while still doing his O-levels, was The Deltas, fronted by guitarist Pete Gage, who later worked with Elkie Brooks in Vinegar Joe. Recalled John: "I also played with my dad in a trio at weddings. We did waltzes and quicksteps and a bit of jazz. It was useful experience which I used throughout my session career and ever since. My father was a really good pianist and as I felt I'd never been as good as him, I took up the organ. I liked the way the notes sustained."

He aspired to go to the Royal College of Music, but instead headed for Soho's Archer Street, a gathering-place for musicians seeking work. He met Jet Harris, formerly of The Shadows, and in 1962 joined Jet and Tony, featuring Harris on guitar and Tony Meehan on drums. They'd had a hit with 'Diamonds' and John, now 17, toured with them for 18 months. In 1963 he met Peter Grant, then driving a van for rock 'n' roller Gene Vincent.

After Jet and Tony, John began doing sessions at Decca, thanks to Meehan's help. Between 1964 and 1968 he recorded with artists including Lulu, Cat Stevens, Shirley Bassey, The Rolling Stones, Rod Stewart, Herman's Hermits, Cliff Richard, Paul and Barry Ryan, Kathy Kirby and Dave Berry; in April 1964 he released a single, an instrumental called 'A Foggy Day In Vietnam'.

ABOVE: Johnny at the Hammond! The drinks are lined up as John Paul Jones plays on Led Zeppelin's private jet, the *Starship*.

John was a backing musician on BBC radio's *Saturday Club* and worked with Dusty Springfield, supporting her at London's Talk Of The Town and arranging tracks on her album *Definitely Dusty*. As an arranger and bass player he worked on Donovan's 'Sunshine Superman' and came to the attention of producer Mickie Most, eventually becoming his musical director. Most shared an Oxford Street office with Grant, then managing the New Vaudeville Band and The Yardbirds, and he and John met again.

John Baldwin became John Paul Jones at the suggestion of Andrew Loog Oldham, the Stones' manager, who saw it on a film poster. Although he now had a stage name there was little opportunity to appear in public, as he spent so many hours in the studio. He was earning good money, but session work six days a week was burning him out. Then his wife read in *Disc* magazine that Page, whom Jones knew from sessions with Donovan and The Yardbirds, was forming a group, and suggested John give him a call. John asked Grant to put him in touch and before long Jones was rehearsing with the New Yardbirds.

When Jones and Page first got together with Bonham and Plant, there was instant chemistry. "We went to a small room in Lisle Street, Soho. We set the amps up and Jimmy said, 'Do you know 'Train Kept A-Rollin' by The Yardbirds?'" John didn't, but it was

a 12-bar blues with a riff in G. "That was the first thing we ever played. It gelled immediately."

Before recording *Led Zeppelin* the band was called in to provide backing tracks for P J Proby's album *Three Week Hero*. Jones was booked as arranger and thought it would be a useful source of income for the new group. Proby's album was released in 1969. Jones: "We had Robert on tambourine and that was the first thing we ever did. Then when we recorded *Led Zeppelin* it was pretty much a recording of our first show. The sound and performance was fantastic. One of the joys of being in the band was you could do anything you liked. It worked and it was so pleasurable. We kept on experimenting and that's why all the Zeppelin albums have a different feel. And it was a really happy band. Everybody thought we were prima donnas, yet there wasn't an ounce of attitude. Page and I had seen it all before and we just didn't want to make any mistakes."

While John was the most laid-back band member ("I'm the boring one", he once remarked), he enjoyed himself on the road just as much. He was described by those working for the band as the wisest and most discreet, but even Jonesy found the tours exhausting and missed his family, to the extent that he considered quitting in 1973. Grant talked him round and he would remain to contribute to albums such as *Physical Graffiti*, *Presence* and *In Through The Out Door*. Most of the time he loved Led Zeppelin ("You get to the point where you enjoy playing so much you just don't want to come off stage") and he was still on stage when they reformed in 2007 for their farewell gig at London's O2 Arena.

LEFT: Conspiratorial glances from Plant and Jones.

BELOW: John Paul Jones with the 1961 Fender Jazz bass he used on most of the band's recordings.

LED ZEPPELIN II

The album sleeve for *Led Zeppelin* depicted the *Hindenburg* in flames at Lakehurst, New Jersey, in 1937. Designed by George Hardie, based on a photo chosen by Page, its impact was so striking that elements were retained for the follow-up. For *Led Zeppelin II*, the sleeve was a drab brown, with a photograph of a group of pilots that had the band members' heads superimposed.

The tracks had been assembled in odd moments on their 1969 US tours. Recording sessions were set up in Los Angeles, New York and London. Mixing took place at A&R Studios in New York under engineer Eddie Kramer, who had worked on the *Electric Ladyland* album with Jimi Hendrix.

Page would later describe putting the album together as "quite insane"; he and Plant had to write in hotel rooms and backstage. However, when it was released in America on October 22, 1969, even the band's hard-bitten attorney Steve Weiss described it as "a masterpiece". Page confessed he had "lost confidence in it" because he had grown over-familiar with the material amid all the overdubbing in different locations. Whatever the difficulties, their hard rock ethos was firmly established and provided just what their army of fans wanted to hear. Advance orders were phenomenal, including half a million in the US, and during its first week it got to Number 15 in the *Billboard* chart, eventually getting to Number One in America and the UK. It sold three million copies in a matter of months.

Much of the excitement was generated by the inclusion of 'Whole Lotta Love'. The menacing opening riff and Plant's cry of 'Woman, you love!' soon established it as part of the soundtrack of the Seventies. Recorded at Olympic Studios with engineer George Chkiantz, it was mixed in New York by Page and Kramer. The full-length version had a long improvised section but was edited down and released as a single in the States, with 'Living Loving Maid' on the B-side. It got to Number 4 in the *Billboard* chart and Number One in Belgium and Germany. It would have been a hit in the UK too, except Grant still didn't want any singles released in Britain. A single release might harm album sales, but there was probably an element of revenge on the UK music industry for not taking his band seriously enough when they started out.

'Whole Lotta Love' makes a grand opening; Plant's cries of "Baby … I'm gonna give you my love!", answered by Page's erotic guitar groans, develop into a thunderous extravaganza. An eerie psychedelic interlude underpinned by Bonham's clever use of cymbals provides an unexpected contrast. This tour de force was successfully covered by British blues man Alexis Korner with his big band CCS, and also performed by the BBC *Top of the Pops* Orchestra as the show's theme tune.

'What Is And What Should Never Be' was a Plant composition recorded at Olympic. He had contributed lyrics to the first album but had not received a credit due to contractual

olems. Here he sings in romantic mood: "And if I say to you orrow". The slow tempo establishes the group's ability to n genres.

he Lemon Song', recorded at the Mystic studio in Los eles, is a traditional blues that allows Plant to indulge in neless teasing: "Squeeze me, baby, until the juice runs n my leg …", A double-tempo section gives Page a chance olo with blistering speed before Jones and Bonham slow gs down. Plant wraps it up with some final squeals of ght before a high-speed finale.

hank You', recorded at Morgan Studios in London and ed in New York, is much more relaxed and tasteful, from moment Plant makes his opening remarks: "If the sun sed to shine I would still be loving you …" Jones gets to e, however, on his Hammond organ, always a subtle but

integral part of the early Zeppelin sound.

'Heartbreaker', recorded and mixed at A&R Studios in New York, is a joint composing effort that features one of Page's most explosive guitar breaks. The song was often used as a set-opener on tour, although later relegated to part of a medley.

'Living Loving Maid (She's A Woman)' is surprisingly poppy, its roots in the Merseybeat era. Page later revealed it was his least favourite track but it remains a moment of calm amid the album's more violent outpourings.

'Ramble On' is very much a vehicle for Plant, whose lyrics seem inspired by *The Lord of the Rings.* Jones' bass lends sensitive support and the drummer relinquishes his kit to play with hands on knees. The full band joins in as Robert sings, "I'm gonna ramble on around the world." The piece fades out under the control of engineer Kramer, who recorded it at Juggy Sound Studios in New York.

While Bonham's expertise was utilized by Page to power up the band when needed, he had plenty of energy in reserve. Increasingly long solos became a highlight of the band's every show, as Bonham battered his drums with his bare hands until he drew blood. 'Moby Dick' was his showcase; the studio version, however, recorded in Los Angeles, lacked the spontaneity of on-stage performances when he would be spurred on by cheering crowds.

'Bring It On Home' celebrates the traditional blues Plant grew to love when he first discovered the early bluesmen. The slow tempo and echoing harmonica reveal the influence of Sonny Boy Williamson, the mood changing abruptly as the rhythm section charges into action. This transforms the piece into a heavy rock interlude before Plant and the harmonica return to wrap up the song and the album.

1970

As album and ticket sales soared, overnight Plant, Page, Bonham and Jones were millionaires, a far cry from playing in pubs for a few pounds a night. Page resided in a boathouse by the Thames at Pangbourne, bought while with The Yardbirds, and drove a Bentley. Plant and his wife invested in a farm in Worcestershire. Bonham drove his brand-new Maserati to his large house in Stourbridge, more spacious than the caravan he previously shared with wife Pat and baby Jason.

1970 began with a British trek that included a sold-out concert at the Royal Albert Hall on January 9. A week later, driving his Jaguar home from seeing visiting American group Spirit, Plant was in a crash, suffered head and facial injuries, and a show in Edinburgh had to be cancelled. He later appeared on stage in a wheelchair.

BELOW: Jimmy Page's acoustic guitar work played a vital role in the Led Zeppelin sound.

By now *Led Zeppelin II* was Number One on both sides of the Atlantic. 'Whole Lotta Love' was played constantly on radio and was at Number 4 in the *Billboard* chart, yet despite many invitations the band avoided TV appearances. In the age before MTV and promo videos TV sound was poor and black-and-white images grainy. However, they did allow their Royal Albert Hall concert to be filmed for posterity.

During February Page began working up material for the third album. As well as editing tapes, he practised guitar three hours a day and even took time out to deny the band was to split:

"There's no reason to split up. There is nothing inherent musically in Led Zeppelin to harm or destroy. There is variety, great freedom and no restrictions on the players whatsoever. In our band everybody respects each other. Everybody plays something to knock each other out. I can't see any split coming. People say to us, 'Now you're established, when are you going to break up?' That's a terrible attitude. We'll carry on and stick together like The Beatles and The Stones."

When everyone was fit and ready the band flew to Copenhagen, where they actually billed themselves as The Nobs to allay complaints from the Zeppelin family. The European tour ended at the Montreux Jazz Festival on March 13. On March 21 they started their fifth North American tour in Vancouver with 27 dates on the schedule.

It was not always a happy outing. There was frequent violence among adolescents hyped up on their perceived heavy metal image. They were greeted with hostility by police and middle-aged Americans who resented their wealth, long hair and flamboyant clothes. In Texas one redneck shouted abuse and pulled a gun. The Vietnam War was polarizing society and tensions were high. Eventually their manager had to hire a posse of bodyguards.

There were brighter moments. In April they were made honorary citizens of Memphis, Tennessee, and fans began

PETER GRANT in association with NANDA and RON LESLEY

★ PROUDLY PRESENT AT BLUESVILLE ★

BATHS HALL - IPSWICH
TUESDAY, NOV. 16
FOR ONE APPEARANCE ONLY

★ ★ ★ ★ ★ ★ ★ ★ ★ ★

INTERNATIONALLY FAMOUS

LED
ZEPPELIN

★ ★ ★ ★ ★ ★ ★ ★ ★ ★

CKETS £1 EACH ON SALE DAILY

AT BATHS HALL BOX OFFICE, IPSWICH (TEL. IPSWICH 53882)
AND ON NIGHT PERFORMANCE 8 — 11 P.M.

they could play at the biggest UK event of the year apart from the Isle of Wight Festival.

Bath turned out to be one of their most memorable concerts. Plant noted: "We went on and knew the next three hours were going to be the ones, as far as holding our heads high. We weren't into it until the acoustic number when we all had a chance to sit down and take a look around. Then it went like clockwork."

There were 200,000 fans packed into the festival site at Shepton Mallet on Sunday, June 28. Robert told them: "We've been away in America and thought it might be a bit dodgy coming back. It's great to be home!" Zeppelin played for over three hours, climaxing with a marathon solo from Bonham. *Melody Maker* reported: "The crowd went wild demanding encore after encore … a total of five!" The mood wasn't quite so ecstatic backstage. Grant discovered some unauthorized filming and recording, and threw a bucket of water over the equipment.

The following month they embarked on a tour of Germany where they played to crowds of 11,000 in Dusseldorf, Essen, Frankfurt and Berlin. Some fans smashed windows demanding "free music" and the band broke attendance records for concerts in the country. In August they began their sixth US tour, in Cincinnati. Page managed to finish mixing their third album in Memphis and Zeppelin played its final concerts of 1970 at Madison Square Garden, in New York, on September 19.

Back in London the group was feted by readers of *Melody Maker*, who voted them Group of the Year, ending The Beatles' long reign. On October 16 they were presented with gold discs by Anthony Grant, Parliamentary Secretary of the Board of Trade, in recognition of their contribution to exports.

On October 23, *Led Zeppelin III* was released, and during the last two months of 1970 the lads took a holiday, interrupted for recording sessions at Island Studios. It was already time to think about the fourth album. Page had in mind an extended piece that would epitomize their ambitions. They were ascending the first rungs on the stairway.

lighting candles, matches and cigarette lighters during concerts to greet their more mellow songs. The tour finished in Phoenix, Arizona, at which point Plant collapsed.

If the band was to finish its third album they would have to take some time off.

Page and Plant headed for a secluded cottage in Snowdonia where Robert had enjoyed many childhood holidays. It was called *Bron-Yr-Aur*, "golden breast" in Welsh. (Although some wags have suggested it actually meant "shut the gate".)

After spending the early part of May in Wales, Plant and Page rejoined the rest of the group to begin recording at Headley Grange, a mansion in Hampshire, followed by more sessions at Olympic during June. In an unusual move, they played two dates in the Icelandic capital Reykjavik, on June 20 and 21, a warm-up for the Bath Festival. It was their second time there and they reportedly turned down offers of US dates worth $200,000 so

LED ZEPPELIN III

Led Zeppelin III was the first album made with time to sit back and contemplate. Plant had suggested going to *Bron-Yr-Aur*, a cottage he had visited as a child, to free their minds from the roar of amplifiers. They hadn't planned to write, but were prepared to see what came out of musical evenings. Recalled Page: "As the nights wore on the guitars came out and numbers were being written."

The music was more varied and relaxed than was usual for a band still dubbed "a heavy metal behemoth" by one US critic. Robert described how they wanted to "get more variety into the act. We're not in one particular bag."

Opener 'Immigrant Song', with lyrics by Plant, was a far cry from the supposed calm of *Bron-Yr-Aur*. "There's a voice at the beginning which somebody thought was a wailing guitar," Page said. "The hiss at the beginning is a tape build-up, and then John Bonham comes in. It's not actually tape hiss, it's more echo feedback." It was laid down at Olympic; and the 'Immigrants' were Vikings seeking new lands, redolent of Robert's continuing interest in ancient legends. It was released as a US single in November 1970, and backed with 'Hey Hey What Can I Do', it made Number 16 in the *Billboard* chart.

'Friends' is another Plant composition. Page: "The idea was to get an Indian music effect with strings. The string players weren't Indian, however, and we had to make some on-the-spot changes. John Paul Jones wrote the incredible string arrangement for this and Robert shows off his great range, reaching incredibly high notes. A friend came into the studio during the recording and it was bloody loud and he had to leave." The theme has echoes of 'Mars' from Holst's *The Planets*.

'Celebration Day' consists mainly of Plant extemporizing over a frantically monotonous riff, a Nineties rave 20 years ahead of schedule. Perhaps it was appropriate that the master tape nearly self-destructed. Page elucidated: "The tape got crinkled in the studio and wouldn't go through the heads, so the end got ruined, but it worked out all right by bringing the synthesizer down in pitch to the voice."

A highlight is the slow-paced yet stirring blues 'Since I've Been Loving You' on which the live band emerges from the fog of edits, synthesizers and strings. Originally destined for *Led Zeppelin II*, it was replaced by 'Whole Lotta Love'. Bonham's finely-balanced drumbeats nail down the tempo, Jones' organ pedals providing the bass line.

'Loving You' has one of Page's finest solos, and one he would reproduce often on stage, but modestly he himself said: "My guitar solo could have been better, but you know, you're never satisfied with a performance. There are those lucky musicians who can play it perfectly every time."

It was back to rock fury for 'Out On The Tiles', inspired by Bonham. When going out for an evening's entertainment he

always chortled a ditty that went: "I've had a pint of bitter and now I'm feeling better and I'm out on the tiles." Jimmy turned the theme into a riff and it became one of Zeppelin's more light-hearted pieces.

The LP's second side showed more of *Bron-Yr-Aur*'s influence. On the folk tune 'Gallows Pole', Page plays banjo (for the first time) and both six- and twelve-string guitars. Page: "'Gallows Pole' was a traditional song from Leadbelly. I first heard it by guitarist Fred Gerlach. He was one of the first white people on Folkways Records to get involved with Leadbelly. We completely rearranged it and changed the verse. Robert wrote a new set of lyrics and John Paul played the mandolin and bass."

'Tangerine' commences with a false start which Page left on as a tempo guide. It's this slightly ramshackle approach which gives the acoustic and more ethnic tracks on the album their more earthy appeal. Page plays pedal steel guitar and Plant supplies both lead vocals and harmonies.

'That's The Way', with its country feel, became a staple of the acoustic set. "It was one of those days after a long walk and we're setting back to the cottage," Page recalled. "We had a guitar with us. It was a tiring walk coming down a ravine and we stopped and sat down. I played the tune and Robert sang a verse straight off. We

'Bron-Yr-Aur Stomp' shows Zeppelin could be equally powerful in rock or acoustic mode. They sound like a supercharged skiffle group; Bonham clatters on spoons and castanets while Jones adds an acoustic five-string fretless bass. Jimmy claimed they used everything, including a kitchen sink, to get an authentic folk flavour. Written as a tribute to Robert's dog Strider, it and had its roots in a piece called 'Jennings Farm Blues.'

The final number was a tribute to Liverpool-born folk legend Roy Harper. Jimmy and Robert first met him at the Bath Festival and selflessly devoted 'Hats Off To (Roy) Harper' to an artist they considered under-rated. Roy later toured with the band as one of their opening acts. Jimmy said: "'Hats Off To (Roy) Harper' came about from a jam Robert and I had one night. Robert had been playing harmonica through the amp and then he used it to sing through. It's a sincere hats-off to Roy because he's a really talented bloke."

Led Zeppelin III was packaged with a unique revolving-wheel cover conceived by Page, based on an old gardening catalogue. While some critics thought the album diffuse and weak, Jimmy explained: "It was another side to us, but we'll never stop doing the heavy things because that comes out naturally when we play. The fourth album should be our best and if it isn't we should give

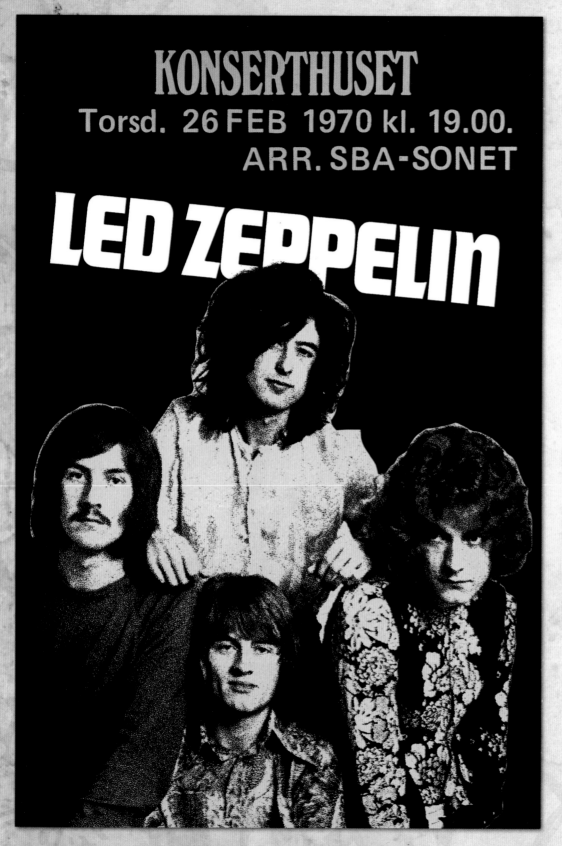

KONSERTHUSET
Torsd. 26 FEB 1970 kl. 19.00.
ARR. SBA-SONET

LED ZEPPELIN

Heriot-Watt University Entertainments
Present
Led Zeppelin
in concert with
Barclay James Harvest
at the USHER HALL EDINBURGH
on Saturday February 7th at 7·30 pm.
REAR STALLS 16'-

please retain this portion. E2

LOCARNO BALLROOM, Sunderland
FRIDAY, 12th NOVEMBER
Led Zeppelin
7 - 12   Licensed Bar till 10.30 p.m.

TICKET : 75p

TOP: A rare ticket to see Led Zeppelin in concert with Barclay James Harvest at the Usher Hall, Edinburgh, Scotland, 1970.

ABOVE: A ticket to see Led Zeppelin in concert at the Locarno Ballroom, Sunderland, England, 1971.

LEFT: A 1970 poster for a date at Sweden's famous blue Concert Hall. The band received gold disks for Swedish sales of *Led Zeppelin II* while on tour there.

RIGHT: Six strings or 12? Jimmy Page in the spotlight with his trusty Gibson EDS-1275.

1971

During 1970 Led Zeppelin did six US tours, at one stage playing six nights a week for a month. Said Bonham: "I was doing a long drum solo every night on tour and my hands were covered in blisters." Even the beefy Peter Grant had to visit a health farm to recover.

Time off the road at least offered a chance to work on the fourth album with less pressure. Adjourning to Headley Grange, their Hampshire rehearsal studio, during January 1971 they utilized The Rolling Stones' mobile studio to record and Page later flew to Los Angeles to mix the tapes.

By the end of February the new album was complete and once more Led Zeppelin hit the road for a British tour, including a visit to Ireland. The show at the Ulster Hall, Belfast, on March 5 was exciting both because of the hysterical welcome – many fans believing Led Zeppelin were American – and because at the height of the Troubles there was a riot going on not far from the venue.

The band were themselves pleased to be reunited; as Plant said after the show, "We're all different personalities but there's a kind of magic when we get together again." He again refuted rumours they were on the verge of breaking up. Fans were rewarded with an especially dynamic performance that kicked off with 'Immigrant Song'. A typical set at this time included 'Heartbreaker,' 'Dazed And Confused' and 'Whole Lotta Love'. Slow blues 'Since I've Been Loving You' was greeted with a storm of applause and barking mad rocker 'Black Dog' got an airing.

The biggest surprise came with an unannounced new ballad featuring a moving vocal performance from Robert and a 12-string guitar interlude from Jimmy. From gentle opening chords to a drum-fuelled climax, the piece progressed through an arrangement that left the audience stunned. Asked to identify the new number, Robert replied: "It's called 'Stairway To Heaven.'" It was the first time audiences had been exposed to what would become one of Led Zeppelin's greatest works, an enduring rock

ABOVE: This (used) ticket from Cologne was to see the band play live on July 16, 1970.

classic and one of the most played tracks on American radio.

An ovation greeted 'Stairway' in both Belfast and at Dublin's Boxing Stadium, where they also performed an unusual version of 'Whole Lotta Love' with Atlantic Records' Phil Carson sitting in on bass. Carson repeated this unscheduled appearance during a trip to Japan when the band quit the stage and left him to twist in the wind, attempting to solo in front of a booing crowd.

During March the band played mostly universities and clubs throughout England, climaxing with a return trip on the 23rd to the Marquee in Soho, where their odyssey had begun back in 1968. Grant had phoned the club's manager Jack Barrie offering Led Zeppelin for one night and at first he refused, thinking it was a hoax. The philosophy behind the "small club" tour was explained by Page. "We were losing contact with people. By doing a tour this way we'll re-establish contact with our audience and re-energize ourselves on their reaction."

A full European tour began in May, ending on July 5 with a troubled show at Milan's Vigorelli Stadium. Here 12,000 fans were attacked with tear-gas and beaten with batons by police and soldiers who over-reacted when the audience stood to cheer after a few numbers. This sparked a full-scale riot, with youths jumping on the stage and climbing into the backstage area. The band escaped through a tunnel and locked themselves into their band room while their road crew tried to salvage equipment.

July wasn't a good month; it was discovered the new album had not been mixed properly at a studio in California and had to be remixed. In August they started their seventh North American tour in Vancouver after two warm-up dates at the Montreux

RIGHT: Robert Plant in characteristic stretched microphone cable posture.

Festival in Switzerland. They played some 20 dates and reputedly earned another million dollars in the process.

In September the group took a holiday in Hawaii after two final tour dates in Honolulu, and at the end of the month a five-date tour of Japan commencing in Tokyo and included a charity show for victims of the Hiroshima atom bombing. However, apart from this well-intentioned gesture the group also began to earn a reputation for mayhem; they were banned for life from the Tokyo Hilton. The band were now used to travelling on a scale few of their age group could contemplate in the era before gap years and backpacking. Robert and Jimmy went on a trip to Thailand, India and Hong Kong.

On November 11 their second UK tour of the year began at Newcastle City Hall. The following day the album sometimes known as *Led Zeppelin IV* was finally released, without a title or any information on the sleeve. On November 20 and 21 Zeppelin performed at the Empire Pool, Wembley; all 19,000 tickets sold in an hour, though some fans grumbled at the price [75p]. They were supported by Bronco, Home and Stone The Crows on two five-hour 'Electric Magic' shows. The tour ended in Bournemouth on December 2 and Atlantic released a single with 'Black Dog' on the A-side in the US. The group resisted great pressure to release 'Stairway To

Heaven' as a single and once again no singles were released in England. The working year ended with a final UK date in Salisbury on December 15.

1971 had been a year of consolidation as well as great progress. It was all part of a whirlwind of activity that left them and their fans breathless. All they knew was that they wanted more.

ABOVE RIGHT: Concert poster from the LA Forum.

BELOW: Unplugged – no Led Zeppelin concert was complete without an acoustic set.

ROBERT PLANT

A mass of curly hair surmounting an exultant grin, bare-chested, in tight jeans, witty, mischievous and blessed with boundless energy, Plant was the perfect figurehead. Steeped in the blues and rock 'n' roll, his charisma, sensitivity and power also made him the perfect foil for Page.

The moment Page and Grant set about devising the band that became Led Zeppelin they knew they wanted a blues singer, but one who could handle a range of material and contribute to the songwriting. At first they considered such fine singers as Steve Marriott, Steve Winwood and Terry Reid, but they were all with other bands or encumbered with contracts. Plant had no baggage and was relatively unknown outside the Midlands, although he had his own band and was already making records.

Robert Anthony Plant was born on August 20, 1948, in Bromwich, Staffordshire. His father was a civil engineer and it was expected that his son would enter the profession. However, inspired by the skiffle boom Robert was quick to pick up all and any available instruments including the kazoo, harmonica and washboard. He listened to all the latest British pop and rock 'n' roll hits, and then a guitar-playing schoolfriend called Terry Foster turned him on to the blues …

"In the early Sixties I was surrounded by English rock," he said. "Some of it was ballsy but a lot of it was half-baked. Then I'd discover the originals on the London American label and a lot more obscure labels coming out of New Orleans. I listened to Snooks Eaglin and then I heard Robert Johnson for the first time when I was 15. It was so sympathetic, almost as if the guitar was his vocal chords. There was tremendous emotional content in the guitar and the vocals. It was the most amazing thing I'd ever heard."

Robert began listening to Buddy Guy and Willie Dixon and absorbing a range of influences, but when he began singing aged 15 he rapidly developed his own kind of power. A tremendous range enabled him to swoop from the highest rock 'n' roll scream to the most intimate interpretation of a ballad.

Like any normal teenager, Robert was as interested in girls and football as music, but he wasn't so enamoured of his lessons and kept on skipping school and joining groups. He began performing at the Seven Stars Blues Club in Stourbridge, playing harmonica with the Delta Blues Band. He'd work out on such favourites

as 'Got My Mojo Working' with Chris Wood, who later joined Traffic, and guitarist Stan Webb, who would form Chicken Shack.

Plant tried folk clubs, too, but found the serious atmosphere too daunting. He needed an enthusiastic audience to perform properly. To placate his family he began studying to be a chartered accountant, but soon gave up. He dared not go home at night because his hair had grown so long; in the event he left home aged 16 to begin a new life as a roving musician.

One of his first gigs was as a "dep" with Andy Long and the Original Jurymen in Leicester, when their singer suffered a bout of laryngitis. He sang with the New Memphis Bluesbreakers, then Black Snake Moan, named after a song by Blind Lemon Jefferson, joined a jazzy outfit called The Banned and then the Crawling

ABOVE: Plant carried on rocking long after Led Zeppelin split up, although his on-stage antics became less hectic.

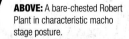

ABOVE: A bare-chested Robert Plant in characteristic macho stage posture.

King Snakes, which featured a drummer called John Bonham.
As Plant's reputation began to spread he was asked to join The
Tennessee Teens, a trio more influenced by Tamla Motown than
Delta-style blues. They changed their name to Listen and in 1966
Robert made his first record when they cut a single, 'You Better
Run'. He also recorded two solo tracks, 'Long Time Coming' and
'Our Song', for CBS.

Listen went on the road, touring with Steampacket, featuring
Rod Stewart and Long John Baldry. By now Plant was able to
sing in a variety of styles, from Stax to Tamla to contemporary
R&B. He was also writing material and formed his own group,
The Band of Joy, but they had a falling-out when he complained
the drummer was slowing down and their manager retorted that
Robert couldn't sing.

Plant then formed a new Band of Joy, which reflected the
trend towards psychedelia, with beads, bells and painted faces.
Influenced by American groups Moby Grape and Love, they
eschewed prevailing British bands such as Cream. Robert drove
the wagon and brought in Bonham on drums. They travelled
to London and played alongside Ten Years After and Fairport
Convention, but there weren't enough gigs to support Robert and
girlfriend Maureen and he had to get a job labouring, including
laying asphalt on the roads of West Bromwich. The other
"navvies" called Robert "the pop singer", but as he explained, the
job "gave me an emergency tax code and big biceps."

The Band of Joy split up and Bonham joined American singer
Tim Rose. Robert was dispirited and disillusioned. He sang with
classic bluesman Alexis Korner and then a little-known outfit
called Hobbstweedle. He was singing with them at a teacher-
training college in Birmingham in July 1968 when he was seen
by Page and Grant, on Terry Reid's recommendation.

When Jimmy first saw the "big guy" with long hair he
thought he was a roadie, but, impressed, invited him to his
home. "It was fantastic," Plant said. "I rummaged through his
record collection and every album I pulled out was something
I really dug. I knew we'd really click." Invited to join The
New Yardbirds, Plant was genuinely thrilled. "The group
really woke me up from inertia. Years with no success can
keep you singing, but it can bring you down an awful lot."

The final verdict came from Page. "When I auditioned
him and heard him sing I immediately thought there must be
something wrong with him because I just couldn't understand
why he hadn't become a big name yet. I thought Robert was
fantastic."

Led Zeppelin had found a singer. Now what they needed was
a drummer, and Plant had the solution; the mate he'd left behind,
somewhere in the Midlands.

Right: Robert Plant was an all-round
performer, and so much more than just a
singer. He played various instruments.

OVERLEAF: Plant wows the massive
Oakland Coliseum crowd, July 23 1977.

BACKSTAGE

LEFT: Electric Magic at Wembley poster for a concert in London, 1971.

ABOVE: A backstage pass from Electric Magic in London, 1971.

"WE'RE ALL DIFFERENT PERSONALITIES BUT THERE'S A KIND OF MAGIC WHEN WE GET TOGETHER."

Robert Plant

RIGHT: A press advertising poster for a concert in Birmingham Town Hall, Birmingham, England, 1970.

FOUR SYMBOLS

Although one of their most productive and well-balanced, the fourth album had a low-key greeting on its release in 1971. A new album was less of a novelty and there was still residue of disappointment at its predecessor; but the critics waiting to sit in judgement were rewarded with an untitled album that revelled in the concept of art sheltering in anonymity and achievement triumphing over celebrity.

Work had started at Island Studios, London, in December 1970, but later the group borrowed The Rolling Stones' mobile studio and moved to Headley Grange, a former Victorian workhouse in Hampshire recommended by Fleetwood Mac, which engineer Andy Johns came to believe was haunted. Plant and Bonham refused to sleep there and decamped to a hotel, but Page liked the atmosphere, especially the acoustics. Among the songs composed at Headley Grange were 'Misty Mountain Hop' and 'The Battle of Evermore', and seated before a blazing log fire (lit because the house was freezing) Plant wrote lyrics to an epic that became known as 'Stairway To Heaven'.

The album was finished in February and the tapes mixed at Sunset Sound studios in Los Angeles. The decision to leave the album untitled was made by Page, reluctant to call it prosaically *Led Zeppelin IV*. It was also decided not to have photos on the cover, as no one could agree who should appear on the front. There were no words either, only an old postcard image of a bearded old countryman bent under the weight of a bundle of rods, contained within a picture frame hung on the wall of a crumbling house. Heavy with yet more symbolism, the inner sleeve was adorned with a charcoal drawing of a hermit holding a lantern, inspired by a tarot card.

Although Grant approved the anonymous cover, the record company men entrusted with promoting the album pronounced it "professional suicide". At a time when the phrase "hype" was in wide circulation among critics, Jimmy explained that they simply wanted to "play down the group's name" and "Led Zeppelin" didn't really mean anything anyway. Only the music mattered.

As the album rocketed to number one the lack of a title certainly caused problems for those publishing the charts, and in the end it was designated either *Untitled* or *Four Symbols*, after the gnomic sigils adorning the label. A feather represented Plant; Bonham was allocated three intertwined rings, signifying strength. Jones' symbol was three leaf shapes linked by a ring and Page's a magical image that looked like "Zoso" indicating his astrological chart, split between Cancer and Capricorn with Scorpio rising.

Having decided that the mixes produced in the States were substandard, the album was remixed in London. The opener, 'Black Dog', one of Zeppelin's heaviest riffs, was inspired by a creature seen wandering around Headley Grange. It was also the name Sir Winston Churchill gave to his fits of depression. Jones devised the theme and an arrangement that included 4/4 and 5/4 time signatures. Page overdubbed four guitar tracks and engineer Johns triple-tracked his rhythm guitars for extra depth. 'Black Dog' was released as a single in America in December 1971 and reached Number 15 in the *Billboard* chart.

'Rock And Roll' celebrated their shared musical roots listening to Little Richard in the 1950s. Bonham sets the mood with hi-hat and snare and Rolling Stones tour manager Ian "Stu" Stewart, who supervised the mobile studio, adds boogie piano. The piece developed when Plant and Page began improvising to break the tension caused by attempting a more difficult piece. 'Rock And Roll' became a stage favourite.

In complete contrast, 'The Battle of Evermore', featuring additional vocals from Sandy Denny of folk rock group Fairport Convention, is an acoustic ballad inspired by Scottish folklore. The melody was devised by Page, using Jones' mandolin, during a session at Headley Grange. They met Sandy during a trip to Los Angeles and performed with her at the Troubadour Club. She died on April 21, 1978.

The fourth track, 'Stairway To Heaven', arrived virtually unheralded and only began to make an impact as it was introduced into live shows. Page's acoustic guitar introduction became a theme all young guitarists aspired to master. He uses a double-necked six- and twelve-string guitar to accompany Plant's airy lyrics and Jones plays wooden recorders, adding a touch of medieval magic. In the

midst of the calm Bonham comes crashing in, followed by Page's storming Fender Telecaster solo, recorded at Island. It was to become the band's anthem, though in later years Plant professed he was embarrassed by the lyrics about a "gilded lady" and tried to avoid singing it at reunions. Page played an instrumental version a a charity concert at the Royal Albert Hall in 1982 and later called i "a glittering thing" summing up all they were trying to achieve.

'Misty Mountain Hop', featuring Jones on electric piano, offers light relief after the drama of 'Stairway' and Plant later revealed it was inspired by an illicit "love-in" he attended.

'Four Sticks', heavily processed and pre-dating electro dance music by 20 years, was intended to be a hypnotic experience inspired by Plant and Page's trip to India. Recorded in one take at Island, it was attempted only once on stage. The title refers to Bonham's use of four drumsticks rather than the usual two.

'Going To California' is from Plant's "Joni Mitchell" phase, featuring Page and Jones on mandolins.

The awesome backbeat of 'When The Levee Breaks' was so powerful it would be sampled by record producers from the 1980s onwards. It was obtained by hanging microphones in Headley Grange's towering stairwell while Bonham played what Plant called "a sex groove." The theme was loosely based on a blues by Memphis Minnie and Page's bottleneck guitar gives it an authentic New Orleans flavour; New Orleans' canal levees really would break in the wake of Hurricane Katrina in 2005.

LEFT: The album turned out some of the band's most popular live numbers, such as 'Black Dog' and 'Stairway To Heaven'.

ABOVE: Robert Plant salutes the crowd from the unusual position of behind a drum kit.

1972

By the early 1970s rock music had become a branch of the entertainment industry that rivalled Hollywood. Scores of new supergroups toured the world and sold albums in their millions. British outfits were at the forefront, notably Pink Floyd, Jethro Tull, Ten Years After, Yes, Deep Purple and ELP, yet the dominant force throughout the decade remained Led Zeppelin.

As well as selling out hundreds of shows, their albums consistently topped the charts. At the start of 1972, single versions of album tracks 'Black Dog' and 'Rock And Roll' from *Four Symbols* permeated the US *Billboard* chart.

The New Year saw the group turn its attention further afield, meeting the demands of distant fans desperate to see them. The only country that proved resistant to their charms was Singapore, refusing them entry because of local bylaws banning men wearing long hair. They had been due to play there in February but instead simply flew on to Australia for a scheduled ten-date tour that began on February 16 in Perth, followed by mainly outdoor shows in Adelaide (19), Melbourne (20), Sydney (27) and Brisbane (29).

There were some problems. In Perth, fans climbed fences to get in and were ejected by police. The show in Melbourne was cut short due to bad weather and Plant was unwell. However, they fitted in a trip to New Zealand and played to 25,000 in Auckland on February 23 – one of the biggest crowds the country had seen at a public event. The show in Brisbane concluded Led Zeppelin's one and only trip to Australasia.

En route to the UK Robert and Jimmy stopped off in India, where they made some experimental recordings with the Bombay Symphony Orchestra; their increasing fascination with Eastern music would later be reflected in several key recordings.

Back in Britain Led Zeppelin began work on recording their fifth album at Olympic Studios, where sessions were held during April and May. They also recorded at Stargroves, Mick Jagger's country home, kitted out with the Stones' mobile studio. In April Robert Plant and wife Maureen celebrated the birth of their son Karac. Then it was back to America for their eighth US tour which opened in Detroit, Michigan, on June 6. They crossed into Canada to play at the Forum in Montreal on June 7 and subsequent dates took them all over the States, from Seattle to Los Angeles and from Chicago to New York, where they appeared at Madison Square Garden on June 21 and 22. The same month they took time out to

BELOW: The Wild Bunch get their motors running and head out on the highway.

ABOVE: By 1972, John Bonham was regularly topping music magazine readers' polls, and was widely thought of as rock's premier drummer.

ABOVE: Led Zeppelin meet and greet the ladies during one of their frequent American tours.

RIGHT: Jimmy Page with an extremely rare 1959 Les Paul Standard – the Holy Grail for many a rock guitarist.

record and mix more tracks for the album to be called *Houses Of The Holy* at Electric Lady Studios in New York.

For the first time in many moons the band members were allowed a two-month holiday during August and September. At the time it seemed perfectly normal for a testosterone-fuelled young band and their entourage to jet around the world and sweat through heart-pounding routines night after night. The relentless schedule would eventually take its toll on their health, but during the period when rock was young and hungry for action there seemed no reason to disappoint all those audiences waiting to see them, not to mention record-buyers lining up at stores to buy anything with Led Zeppelin on the label.

On October 2 they began a second Japanese tour in Tokyo with the first of two sets at the Budokan. During their trips to Tokyo and Osaka, the group enjoyed indulging in their new hobby of photography, having bought the latest Japanese cameras. Their merrymaking on a grand scale continued unabated. When asked about their allegedly wild behaviour on the road to alleviate the boredom of staying in hotels, Robert replied: "Of course, it's usually one of our roadies that rides along with us that gets us a bad reputation with his ... shenanigans." The final show was in Kyoto on October 10 where they played a relatively short set that included 'Stairway To Heaven'. They returned to Europe to play two dates at Montreux Casino on October 28 and 29.

By November the fifth album was completed, but would not be released for another three months. British fans were placated

when Zeppelin announced a full UK tour. As soon as the news was announced some 100,000 tickets for all the shows sold out in one day. The tour began on November 30 at Newcastle City Hall and they went on to Glasgow, Manchester, Cardiff, Birmingham and Brighton. Reaching London near Christmas they played two dates at Alexandra Palace on December 22 and 23. These were their biggest indoor concerts in the UK thus far, and went down a storm. The tour would continue into January 1973.

It was this sort of demanding schedule that led Bonham to proclaim: "There are times when you sit down and say, 'I wanna go home.' It's not the playing, which I could do all day; it's the surroundings ... and getting blisters." Their life on the road meant they got less time to be with their families and, said Jones: "I get hell for going on tour. Once I had all the time in the world and no money. Now I have the money but no time."

1972 had been a less dramatic year, in the sense that it was the first since their inception in which they hadn't released an album. They had also tried to spend less time on the road. Nevertheless they had achieved some more "firsts", including their conquest of Australia and New Zealand.

The band faced the next year with one of their most controversial albums in the pipeline and planning an exciting new venture – a full-length feature film capturing the band in action. They also intended beefing up their live shows with special effects that would see Led Zeppelin once again ahead of the competition in the world of stadium rock – a genre they were helping to define.

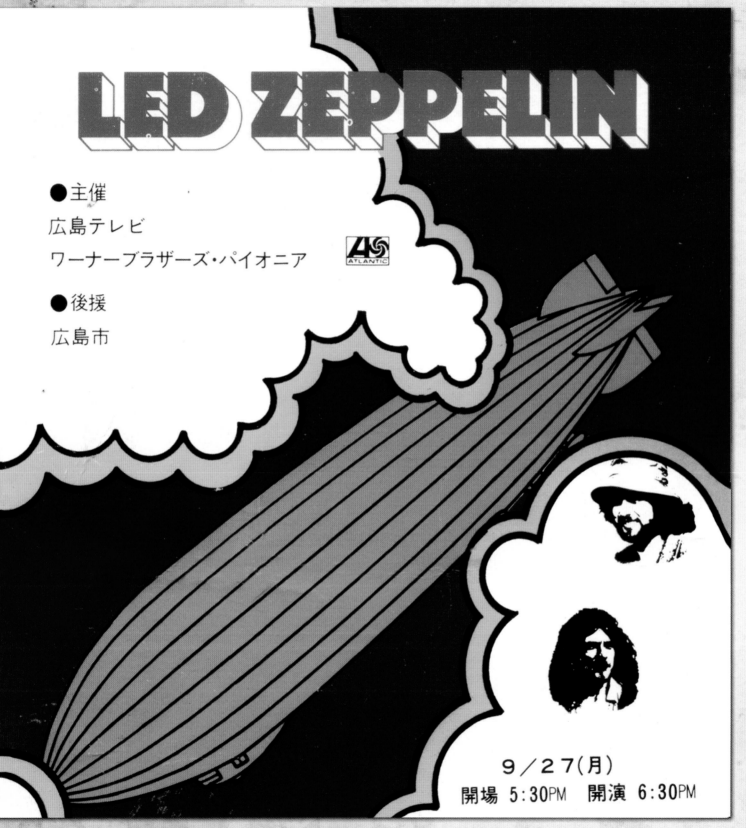

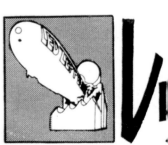

"IT'S USUALLY ONE OF THE ROADIES THAT RIDES ALONG WITH US THAT GETS US A BAD REPUTATION WITH HIS ... SHENANIGANS."

Robert Plant

LEFT: A rare flyer for a concert in Tokyo, Japan in 1972.

1973

Led Zeppelin was a truly huge band, known all around the world for their concerts, music and antics. They were the epitome of popular music at the time and were worshipped by their fans.

The year saw the scale of the band's operations grow exponentially, as enormous crowds were attracted to increasingly elaborate shows. Zeppelin won awards, topped polls and embarked on new projects. At the same time, headlines gave the first hints of strange undercurrents.

They began 1973 fulfilling dates on the UK tour begun the year before. It wasn't all smooth sailing. On January 2 the Bentley transporting Plant and Bonham to Sheffield City Hall broke down and they nearly missed the show. Then Plant succumbed to influenza and some shows had to be rescheduled. The tour finished in Preston on January 30.

The album was delayed by arguments over the sleeve. Eventually released on March 26, *Houses Of The Holy* had an eye-catching gatefold cover depicting naked girls crawling over rocks, but minus a band name or title. This scarcely mattered. Within days it was Number One in both the UK and US, and went gold in Germany even before release.

Discussing the album, Plant claimed: "All our albums are different and in four years we've covered all sorts of ground. We have a track called 'The Crunge' which is really funny, and we've also written a reggae number, which I'd like to put out as a single." In the event the song, 'D'Yer Mak'er', was released in the States and by December was Number 20 in the *Billboard* chart.

A European tour commenced in Copenhagen on March 3, winding up in Paris on April 1 and 2 with two nights at the Palais de Sport. During April the band was busy rehearsing a stage show involving lots of special effects. Their ninth US tour opened on May 4 in front of 50,000 at the Atlanta Braves' stadium. An excited city mayor called the show "the biggest thing to hit Atlanta since *Gone With The Wind*." But even this wasn't their biggest audience. The following day they entertained 56,800 ecstatic fans at the Tampa Stadium, Florida, breaking the record for a gig by a single group set by The Beatles at Shea Stadium in 1965.

Grant proudly told the *Financial Times* Led Zeppelin expected to earn $30 million during 1973; Atlanta earned them $250,000 and Tampa Stadium grossed $309,000. Audiences were transfixed by elaborate stage sets by Showco of Dallas, Texas. Thirty tons of light and sound equipment included strobe lights, spinning mirrors and dry ice machines. The Zeppelin entourage journeyed across the States like a wagon train rolling west, while the band flew in a private Boeing 707, *Starship 1*. The tour concluded

with another sold-out show at the Los Angeles Forum on June 3.

It was clear to Grant that Zeppelin would become a major part of rock history and the experience should be filmed for posterity. Work began on a movie, to be called *The Song Remains The Same*, the title of the new album's opening track. Directed by Joe Massott, a friend of Page's girlfriend Charlotte Martin, filming began on July 18 with a crew covering gigs in Baltimore, Boston and Pittsburgh, plus three nights at Madison Square Garden in New York on July 27, 28 and 29, where engineer Eddie Kramer deployed a 24-track mobile recording unit. Massott planned something more than a static "rockumentary", presenting each band member in personality-driven "fantasy" sequences, intercut with concert footage.

Real-life events began to upstage any Zeppelin fantasies. After the second night at Madison Square Garden, tour manager

Richard Cole and attorney Steve Weiss put $186,700 of wages money into a safe deposit box at the Drake Hotel in Manhattan. Overnight the money went missing. An after-show party was scheduled where gold discs were presented, but when Press and TV asked about the alleged robbery the band refused to discuss it. To make matters worse, Peter Grant was subsequently arrested for hitting a photographer.

Cole was cleared of any involvement in the theft, but the money was never found. From then on the band attracted unwelcome publicity and suffered more than their share of bad luck. Page had been ill during the tour and strained a finger, affecting his playing. Back in the UK, he announced he just wanted to go to sleep. He thought they would start work on another new album, but yearned for a break. "I can't remember when we weren't working. It's been an incredible tour but we're all terribly worn out."

In September Plant was voted Top Male Singer in *Melody Maker*'s annual readers' poll. The band started work on the successor to *Houses Of The Holy* at Plumpton Place, Jimmy's

18th-century residence set in 50 acres in East Sussex. He also bought Boleskin House near Loch Ness in Scotland, once owned by the occultist Aleister Crowley. As work progressed on *The Song Remains The Same*, a fantasy sequence was filmed there in December, with Page as a hermit climbing ice-covered rocks in the moonlight. Sequences filmed during October depicted Plant as an Arthurian knight on a quest for a princess and Bonham driving a dragster at Bedfordshire's Santa Pod Raceway. Jones was a masked brigand terrorizing a village before returning to his Sussex family home. Even Grant was roped in, driving a vintage car and posing as Al Capone, with Cole his henchman.

By the end of 1973 thousands of feet of film awaited editing. It would prove a difficult task. The band sometimes felt out of their depth with the project; they were more at home at Headley Grange, where they continued work on the sixth album.

One of the demo tracks was a strange, Eastern-sounding theme Grant privately thought "a dirge". In fact, it was the first rumblings of one of their most celebrated tracks, 'Kashmir'. After an exhausting year, the creative juices were flowing again.

HOUSES OF THE HOLY

The first track, 'The Song Remains The Same' is an outstanding performance that lights up the whole album. Its world-weary wisdom conveyed in contemplative lyrics amid the grandeur of a commanding theme, it represents Zeppelin at its best. However, the rest of the album is not always as successful, giving the impression of a compilation of ideas that took the band's fancy in the studio.

Even so, *Houses Of The Holy* has some vintage material and splendid performances, notably by Jimmy Page whose guitar work is inspired. Released on March 28, 1973, it went straight to Number One in both the US and UK.

Again there was no title or name on the cover. The orange-hued gatefold LP sleeve was a tinted photograph of eleven naked young girls climbing over a rocky landscape, the Giant's Causeway in Northern Ireland. On the inner sleeve a naked man holds up one of the girls in front of a ruined castle.

Despite the intriguing imagery, the cover didn't really relate to the music. It was, however, their first album to have a full title. Houses of the Holy was said to refer to the venues where Zeppelin played, as they communicated with their mass following. The song 'Houses of the Holy' didn't appear on the album but was featured later on *Physical Graffiti*.

When work began the band had no set ideas and waited to see what would come out in the studio. Some tracks evolved from jam sessions that seemed like fun at the time, but there was no master plan or sustained system of songwriting. Although it looked like a concept album, it proved disjointed and the recorded sound didn't have quite the impact of *Four Symbols*.

'The Song Remains The Same' sets off at a blistering tempo, slowing down briefly to allow Robert's vocal extemporization as he muses on his travels from California to Calcutta and beyond. As the speed rises again Page unleashes a marvellous solo while the bass sustains the underlying theme. The vocals are processed to raise the pitch, so it sounds as if Plant is inhaling helium from a party balloon. The piece is so carefully structured it was originally entitled 'The Overture' and was to have featured as an instrumental until lyrics were added.

'The Rain Song' is gentle and slow, acoustic guitars supporting Robert's vocals. His voice glows with kindly warmth as he sings, "Speak to me only with your eyes, it is to you I give this tune." Jones adds a Mellotron to the backing, giving a suitably eerie and mournful effect. This unique keyboard instrument relied on a system of tapes to provide sampled strings and was very popular with such groups as Genesis and The Moody Blues during the 1970s. 'The Rain Song' is well-crafted pop, and a far cry from 'Communication Breakdown' – as was intended.

'Over The Hills And Far Away' sustains the low-key mood with a performance that wouldn't have been out of place in a folk club.

Acoustic guitar chords chime as Robert intones sadly, "Many have I loved, many times been bitten …" Zeppelin sound like a different band, closer to the West Coast scene of the late Sixties, with elements of country rock surfacing amidst the choppy, accentuated beats. In true Zeppelin fashion, however, they move forward into different grooves before a tricky coda fades out, only to return. Released as a single in the US in May 1973, it peaked at 51 in the *Billboard* chart.

Next comes 'The Crunge', a spontaneous jam built over a funky beat Bonham began laying down as a studio warm-up. Jones joins in on bass and Page improvises in a style James Brown would have approved of, except that the beat crosses over repeatedly, making it, in Page's words, "undanceable". Jimmy uses his Fender Stratocaster's tremolo arm for a special effect every few bars. Robert's lyrics sound like a latter-day rap as he refers obliquely to his favourite singers, Otis Redding and Wilson Pickett. It was intended to be fun, although not all fans approved.

'Dancing Days' is one of the album's better tracks, blending Eastern styles with rock influences. A grating, insistent guitar riff launches a melody Page and Plant picked up on a trip to Bombay, although they could have heard similar music in the curry-houses of Birmingham. Recorded at Stargroves and mixed at Electric Lady studio in New York, it has one of Plant's more unusual vocals.

'D'Yer Mak'er' (a pun on 'Jamaica') was a trip into reggae, a first for the band and the result of Robert's keen interest in different ethnic music forms. Bonham's drum sound is excellent, although his "heavy" approach doesn't necessarily suit the reggae rhythm. Surprisingly, it got to Number 20 in the *Billboard* singles chart in November 1973.

'No Quarter' is a much more interesting arrangement, built on Jones' piano and full of intriguing overtones. Robert sings about "The dogs of doom … howling" as Page locks into some jazzy improvisation pre-dating the sound of such latter outfits as the Cinematic Orchestra. It became a showcase number and was performed at the band's Earls Court shows in 1975.

Final track 'The Ocean' kicks off with Bonham chanting a gruff introduction before setting up a driving backbeat. With Plant laughing and singing it's a gleeful performance enlivened by a sudden switch into a swing tempo that enables Page to solo with joyous freedom. 'The Ocean' in question was the vast audience the band performed to every night on tour. In his final lines Robert declaims, "I'm singing all my songs to the girl who won my heart … she's only three years old and it's a real fine way to start," a touching line dedicated to his daughter Carmen.

When some reviews were less than complimentary Plant responded: "So there's some buggers that don't like the album. Well, God bless 'em. I like it, and there's a few thousand other buggers that like it too."

THE EFFECT IS SHATTERING...

ABOVE: Bill poster for the *Houses of the Holy* album.

LEFT: Jimmy Page takes a bow on stage, once again.

BELOW: A ticket for the concert at Budokan Hall, Tokyo, Japan in 1972.

LED ZEPPELIN

Led Zeppelin began in a small, stuffy rehearsal hall, in London, late 1968. "Four of us got together in this two by two room and started playing. Then we knew - we started laughing at each other. Maybe it was from relief, or maybe from the kowledge that we knew we could groove together. But that was it. That was just how well it was going". Jimmy Page, master guitarist, former Yardbird, was watching his thoughts, his ambitions, his concealed desires as a musician, take shape in a new supergroup, Led Zeppelin.

"The statement of our first two weeks together is our album. We cut it in 15 hours, and between us wrote 8 of the tracks. Our main problem was knowing what channel to take it along musically. Everyone in the group had such a high musical content we thought each of us would be into our own thing. But it all fell together.

"We'll probably always be faced with the fact that individually, each member could cut his own album going in his own direction and it would be great. But all those ideas in one outfit, well , thats pretty fantastic too".

The formation of Led Zeppelin was on easy task. When it became generally known that Jimmy Page was putting a group together, he was indudated with calls from musicians all over the country. When Yardbirds finally split up in the summer of 1968, Jimmy was ready to take bass player Chris Dreja with him into Led Zeppelin.Chris eventually backed out of the arrangement, choosing instead to go into management.

"When I joined the Yardbirds, my main reason was to give myself the opportunity of playing my own music. Before that, my only interest was session work. I began to feel limited not being able to express myself. When I left, it was for almost exactly the same reasons. The group split because everyone began to feel the need to go in his own direction. The pity is, there would have still been great potential".

It was all down to Jimmy Page, alone, on a one man campaign to make himself heard. As a session guitarist he was, and still is, one of the finest in England, contributing his works to tracks by such stars as the Stones, Donovan, and latterly, Joe Cocker, who took the Beatles' "With A Little Help From My Freinds" to such a smash.

ABOVE AND RIGHT: A 1973 souvenir programme, folded with signatures of all band members inside – as well as a few typos too.

"I was working on the Dinovan album, "Hurdy Gurdy Man" with John Paul Jones who did some of the arrangements. He asked if I could Use a bass guitarist in Led Zeppelin. John is an incredible arranger and musician. He didn't need me for a job, but he felt the need to express himself and figured we could do that together.

"Sessions are great, but you can't get into your own thing. Both myself and John felt that in order to give what we had to offer we had to have a group. He wanted to be part of a group of musicians who could lay down some good things".

"I can't put a tag to our music . Every one of us has been influenced by the blues, but it's one's interpretation of it and how you utilize it. I wish someone would invent an expression, but "I want us to be raw and basic. That was the whole thing that made the Yardbirds happen. To go into your own thing is fine, but it has to be a form of experimentation that evolves from a basic sound that everyone else knows and can relate to."

It took two years for Led Zeppelin to emerge. The name was conceived by Jimmy Page when he was still with the Yardbirds and each member of the group took a shot at recording on his own. Jimmy penned "Beck's Bolero" for Jeff Beck. Today it's a Beck standard, then, it was a track on which the Who's Keith Moon played drums. "When we were kicking around group names, I suddenly remembered Led Zeppelin which I had come up with at that time."

That too would have been a supergroup. but every musician to his own bag, and for Jimmy Page, it's John Paul Jones, John Bonham and Robert Plant to make Led Zeppelin an example of great music. And this is a group that won two standing ovations and two encores on their first date in London, with only six hours of rehearsal behind them.

It's the greatest trip any selection of musicians can take their audience on, the greatest feeling of being into a scene, one which America is ready and waiting for. On this, their latest tour, every ticket at enery Theatre was sold within four hours of the announcement. Considering this a is thirty day package of the entire country it must give some idea of their popularity.

"I WANT US TO BE RAW AND BASIC."

Jimmy Page

1974

Fire-eaters and semi-naked wenches featured at the wildest party Led Zeppelin threw during a year of celebrations, holidays and new ventures. 1974 was their first period in six years with no tours or record releases planned.

ABOVE: After five manic years, John Bonham was glad of a well-earned rest in 1974.

LEFT: Robert Plant contemplates the state of his locks.

They certainly deserved a break, and enjoyed the novelty of being at home with their wives and girlfriends, but they didn't break with music entirely; one project in particular occupied Jimmy Page and manager Peter Grant.

The concept of the "artist-owned label" had grown during an era when artists fought to gain control of their music and money. Elton John had Rocket, The Beatles owned Apple and The Rolling Stones their own eponymous label. Now Led Zeppelin entered the fray. Their contract with Atlantic had expired; they wanted to broaden their activities by setting up their own label, Swan Song, to be distributed by Atlantic.

In typically oblique fashion, they eschewed flashy offices in a shining tower block in favour of dusty rooms above the British Legion headquarters in London's New King's Road. With cheap furniture and few staff, it gave no hint of the band's immense wealth, perhaps to discourage visiting artists from imagining they too might be in line for a fortune.

The label name had been the subject of heated debate; suggestions included Slag, Eclipse, De Luxe, Stairway and Zeppelin Records. Swan Song was originally intended as the

name of an acoustic guitar track, then an album title, until finally applied to the label. The chosen logo depicted two graceful swans, similar to those on the lake at Jimmy's house.

Among its first signings was Scots singer Maggie Bell, formerly of Stone The Crows, who was managed by Grant. Long-established R&B band The Pretty Things were given a contract as was rock 'n' roll producer, artist and writer Dave Edmunds. The most successful, however, proved to be Bad Company, a lusty young group featuring former Free vocalist Paul Rodgers. A second office was set up in Manhattan, where it was hoped major stars would be secured.

That month the group convened to start work on their sixth album, with sessions at Headley Grange. Jones was back on board, having considered quitting due to the strain of touring and becoming choirmaster at Winchester Cathedral. Grant succesfully convinced him to stay.

Although no Zeppelin gigs were scheduled, they had fun turning up at other people's and sitting in; one memorable night Page joined old pal Roy Harper on stage at London's Rainbow Theatre.

On May 10, Swan Song Records was officially launched with two lavish receptions for the media and music industry. The first, at

the Four Seasons restaurant in New York, reputedly cost $10,000. As Atlantic's promotions department couldn't find any swans they hired a flock of geese; Grant was furious that they thought nobody would notice. When two were chased outside by Bonham and Richard Cole, they were run over by a car.

The second was in Los Angeles, at the Bel Air Hotel. On the flight Grant and his 12-strong party were mocked, berated and sworn at by a drunken fellow-passenger who eventually produced a gun, demanding to know how "hippies" could afford to fly first-class. On landing he was arrested by the FBI and the somewhat shaken group continued on their way.

Safely in Hollywood, party guests included comic legend Groucho Marx, Micky Dolenz of The Monkees and Rolling Stone Bill Wyman. During the visit John Paul Jones was introduced to Elvis Presley, an honour repeated the following year for the rest of the band.

Swan Song got a big boost when Bad Company's debut album topped the US charts and single 'Can't Get Enough' was a hit on both sides of the Atlantic. The first British release was The Pretty Things' album *Silk Torpedo*. Label managers yearned for a major artist such as John Lennon but the biggest act remained, of course, Led Zeppelin, five of whose albums were on Swan Song.

Grant was offered a chance for the group to headline a one-day festival at Knebworth in July and a date at the Munich Festival on August 29. He declined; they were too busy concentrating on the label, their new album and a film.

The band had begun losing interest in the movie after seeing incomplete rushes, and the project was taken over by Australian director Peter Clifton. He had made films for Australian TV, about Chuck Berry and US soul acts visiting London in the 1960s, which had impressed the band. He took them to Shepperton Studios for more filming.

In July mixing sessions were held at Olympic Studios. As they had quite a few tracks left over from previous albums, it was decided the next should be a double. Release was scheduled for the following year.

The summer saw many Zeppelin sideshows. Jones formed a group with Dave Gilmour of Pink Floyd to back Roy Harper at a free concert in Hyde Park. In September Page jammed with Bad Company during their US tour, and the band went to see Crosby, Stills, Nash and Young at Wembley Stadium.

On October 31 Swan Song held a party at Chislehurst Caves in the south London suburbs to celebrate *Silk Torpedo*'s release. Guests included Zeppelin, Bad Company and The Pretty Things; booze flowed like water and entertainment was provided by fire-eaters and semi-naked serving wenches. Their inspiration was the notorious Hell Fire Club, which in the 18th century held orgiastic revels in caves at High Wycombe. Those attending Zeppelin's 20th-century version remained hung over for days.

Once recovered, Led Zeppelin announced double album *Physical Graffiti* would be released on November 29 and that a US tour would begin in January. As rehearsals began in earnest at an Ealing theatre, Page commented: "1974 didn't really happen. 1975 will be much better."

TOP RIGHT: An invitation to Led Zeppelin's exclusive 1974 Halloween Party.

RIGHT: Jimmy Page readies himself for a heavy duty year ahead.

Do what thou wilt . . .
But know by this summons
That on the night of the Full Moon
of 31st October, 1974
Led Zeppelin
request your presence
at a
Halloween Party
to celebrate
Swan Song Records'
first U.K. album release
'Silk Torpedo'
by
The Pretty Things
in
Chislehurst Caves,
Chislehurst, Kent.
Celebrations will commence
at 8.00 p.m. . . .

Swan Song Records
by Atlantic Records

1975

For British fans, 1975 was the year when Zeppelin dominated London's Earls Court for five sensational nights – May 17, 18, 23, 24 and 25 – regarded by many as their finest hours. They presented their full American production, unleashed new material and entranced a new generation of fans. They also released one of their most important albums.

The year began with shows in Rotterdam (January 11) and Brussels (12). Then Page, hurrying to a rehearsal, broke his left ring finger in a train door at London's Victoria Station. Grant feared the tenth US tour might be in jeopardy, and they'd sold 700,000 tickets. However, Page was back for the opening night at the Metro Sports Centre, Minneapolis, on January 18, though he couldn't bend notes. 'Dazed And Confused' was replaced with 'How Many More Times' to protect Page's finger.

Although the tour was a success, fears were growing about the band's financial security. The UK tax rate on high earners was then 87 per cent. The group had to become "non-resident" and move abroad for a year; Bonham and Plant were particularly unhappy, but the band moved to France or Switzerland when they weren't in the States. Grant stayed in America, renting a house on Long Island.

The 1975 US tour exceeded all expectations. There were riots in Boston even before the band hit town. The show used a 70,000W PA system, laser-equipped lighting rig and a crew of 44 technicians. Plant caught 'flu in Chicago and struggled through shows in Cleveland and Indianapolis. A date in St Louis on January 26 had to be cancelled. Robert holed up in a Chicago hotel while the others flew to LA for 24 hours' leave.

As the *Starship* had its own bar and an electric piano, they were able to party on. The next day they flew to North Carolina for a show at Greensboro Coliseum (January 29), where 500 youths unable to get tickets tried to storm the venue and stoned their limos. When the drivers tried to abandon the band Grant commandeered a Cadillac, grabbed his charges and drove through the mob out of the arena, heading for the airport. After racing through red lights at 70mph he completed several laps of honour around the waiting plane, tyres screeching, then kicked the car, complaining it wasn't as fast as his Bentley.

During breaks in touring the band got up to some of their more notorious hotel escapades, including stuffing Bonham's wardrobe with mudsharks, fished from the ocean, which fell out on an unsuspecting maid. Wild parties staged by promoter Bill Graham ended in food fights and mayhem. Bonham was even observed riding a motorbike along a corridor at the Hyatt "Riot" House in West Hollywood.

They could afford such mischief. In two months Led Zeppelin grossed $5 million. A highlight was playing six concerts to 120,000 fans in the New York area, including three nights at Madison Square Garden, with Mick Jagger and David Bowie in the house. Rod Stewart went to one of three shows at Nassau Coliseum, which completed stage one of the tour on February 14. It ended with three shows at the Los Angeles Forum, concluding on March 27.

ABOVE: On the road yet again – Led Zeppelin hit the US for the tenth time since 1969.

LEFT: Bonzo was a hard taskmaster for any drum kit.

During the trip Grant and the band went to see Elvis in Las Vegas. He stopped the show to announce that Led Zeppelin was in the audience and invited them back to his suite for a 20-minute visit that lasted two and a half hours. An exhausted Grant dropped his 18 stone on to a sofa – and the legs of Elvis' father Vernon. Grant apologized to Mr Presley and then to Elvis. Elvis responded, "Stick around, kid; you might get a permanent job."

Physical Graffiti was released on February 24, instantly going gold, then platinum, and topping the *Billboard* chart. Their entire back catalogue was revived and all their albums charted again.

In April Page, Plant and Grant flew to New York on Swan Song business and Jimmy began mixing the soundtrack for *The Song Remains The Same*. In May the five nights at Earls Court drew 85,000 people. Promoter Mel Bush could have sold twice as many.

TOP: Although tame by moden standards, Led Zeppelin's stage shows were suitably opulent for the world's biggest rock band.

Reportedly, 51,000 tickets sold in two hours and the rest went over the weekend.

For their first UK appearances since 1973 Dallas-based Showco flew in the equipment and employed a 15-man crew. A video screen enabled the audience to see the band close up. They performed five numbers from the new album, notably the fast and funky 'Trampled Underfoot', while 'Dazed And Confused' went down a storm. Page, wreathed in smoke pierced by green laser beams, flailed his guitar with the bow to produce eerie howls around the cavernous venue. 'Moby Dick' and 'Whole Lotta Love' concluded shows presenting Zeppelin at the peak of their powers: yet within a couple of months they faced disaster.

Plant took his family to Morocco, met Page and drove across the Sahara in a Range Rover. They drove back to Europe and met the group in Switzerland where Grant was planning the next US tour, due to start on August 23 and to include South American dates. After attending the Montreux Jazz Festival, Page and Plant went to the Greek island of Rhodes.

Page left for Italy on August 3; the following day Plant's rental car hit a tree. Maureen's skull was fractured; Robert broke his ankle and elbow. Karac and Carmen, in the back, were unhurt. All were

ABOVE: Led Zeppelin at Earl's Court – for some, the greatest rock concert evert staged.

taken by truck to hospital and then flown home. Maureen was concussed and Robert told he couldn't walk for six months. The tour was cancelled and Robert moved hastily to Jersey to avoid punitive taxes.

Later the band moved to Malibu to plan a new album. During recording at Musicland Studio in Munich, Robert fell; not until December was he able to walk again without a crutch. The year that began with such high hopes had ended on a sombre note.

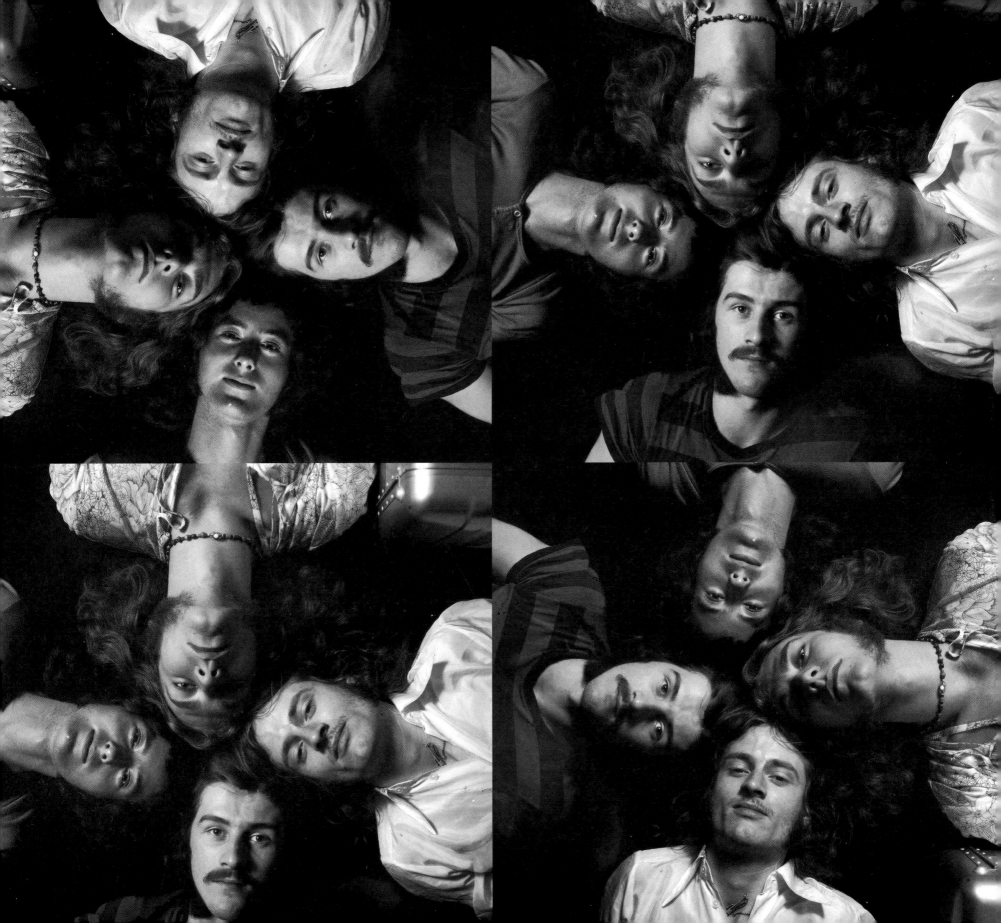

PHYSICAL GRAFFITI

Physical Graffiti was one of Led Zeppelin's most impressive works and a step towards achieving their ambition of creating the ultimate album. Amidst a mass of material on a double LP, not all of the tracks matched the much admired 'Kashmir'. However, it was altogether Zeppelin's strongest showing in some years and restored the faith of fans and critics alike.

The bold confidence was reflected both in the music and the imaginative cover art. It was first Zeppelin release on Swan Song and the band's name and album title was clearly displayed. Record buyers were intrigued by a cover that depicted the windows and blinds typically observed in a New York brownstone tenement building. With holes cut in the cardboard sleeve it was possible to slide the inner bags to reveal surreal images and activities going on inside the "apartments." Jimmy Page later described the effect as: "A Peeping Tom's delight."

Physical Graffiti was released on February 24, 1975 with 15 tracks including eight that had been recorded at Headley Grange the previous year, using the late Ronnie Lane's mobile studio. There were also seven songs culled from the archives and dating back to the days of *Led Zeppelin III*.

It was Zeppelin's longest studio album. Because they only had enough new material for one and a half LPs, they decided to top it up with older recordings to complete the double set. When they met up to start work for the first time in six months it was after a period of uncertainty about their future. They had all been exhausted by lengthy American tours and needed time to recover and recharge their batteries.

Jimmy Page had spent some time at his home, working up ideas and themes. These were gradually pieced together and fleshed out during sessions that evolved out of studio warm-ups. Sometimes they'd simply play their old favourites to relax. Then a new piece would evolve and take on its own life.

The opening track, 'Custard Pie' immediately grabs the listener with its emphatic guitar riff and pounding back beat drums. Robert slips easily into his more raucous mode; a style that would inspire many a future heavy metal singer. John Paul Jones plays electric clavinet behind a theme rooted in Blind Boy Fuller's 'I Want Some Of Your Pie'.

The strong pulse is maintained on 'The Rover', a seminal Seventies rock tune born out of an early acoustic version. It's a unified band performance with Robert's vocals dominating while Jimmy takes a relatively brief and melodic solo. The rock jam that develops in the final chorus harks back to the days of Eric Clapton's Cream.

The third track 'In My Time Of Dying', is an 11-minute marathon that commences with a slow paced bluesy introduction from Jimmy setting the scene. His slide guitar licks are redolent of Southern swamps and cotton fields. Robert intones plaintively "In

my time of dying … as Bonzo interjects thunderous support from the depths of his drum kit. The whole piece picks up tempo and evolves into a spontaneous celebration as if the band are playing a "live" club gig. Page revealed later that the piece lacked a proper ending and they simply jammed their way towards a coda. In many ways this represented *le vrai* Zeppelin.

'Houses of the Holy' should perhaps have appeared on the 1973 album of the same name. The title refers to their "congregation" of fans and the spiritual atmosphere they generated at concerts. A sturdy rocker, Robert sings lustily against a barrage of riffs. The number had its origins in the 1972 sessions held at the Olympic Studios in Barnes.

One of the biggest pleasures and surprises of *Physical Graffiti* is the launch into the realms of funk displayed on the irresistible and hypnotic 'Trampled Underfoot'. This gem is essentially a romp over a series of funky riffs with a stomping beat generated by Mr. Bonham. It takes on a life of its own as John Paul Jones launches into a jazzy electric piano solo, complete with cliff hanging breaks. When it jerks back into the beat again the effect is electrifying. It's one of those numbers that doesn't want to stop, a feeling echoed by the audience at Earls Court when they first heard it performed "live" in 1975.

As if this wasn't enough the exciting 'Trampled Underfoot' is hotly pursued by the sensational 'Kashmir' a theme so dramatic it has been used in many a theatrical setting including TV's *The X Factor* talent show

in 2009. Taken at slow and ponderous tempo, the menacing aura that surrounds this Eastern flavoured magnum opus is so unusual it aroused some puzzlement among the band's closest advisers. They referred to it as "the dirge" until its power and majesty began to take effect.

Over the coming years 'Kashmir' came to surpass even 'Stairway To Heaven' as the band's greatest set piece and all the band members proclaimed it was a highlight of the band's career. The concept began life when Robert composed some lyrics during a long and bumpy holiday trip across the Sahara Desert. It was originally called 'Driving To Kashmir' – his dream destination. The mood it engendered revealed Plant and Page's increasing fascination with both Moorish and Indian music. The theme was worked up on demo recordings laid down by Page and Bonham and later arranged by John Paul Jones. The addition of an orchestra into the mix of guitars and drums worked perfectly.

'In the Light' that follows is another atmospheric piece that develops more slowly and is predicated on John Paul Jones use of a VCS synthesizer. It was recorded at Headley Grange and was never performed on stage due mainly to technical difficulties. But it remains an intriguing example of Zeppelin in cutting edge experimental mode. Plant sings of self revelation and the need for "the light" to exert a life balance.

'Bron-Yr-Aur' is different from the 'Bron-Y-Aur Stomp' that appeared on *Led Zeppelin III*. It features Jimmy Page playing solo Martin guitar on a two-minute acoustic instrumental that dates back to 1970. A delightful performance, it provides a perfect interlude between band performances, heightening the effect that *Physical Graffiti* is a self-contained concert and not just an album.

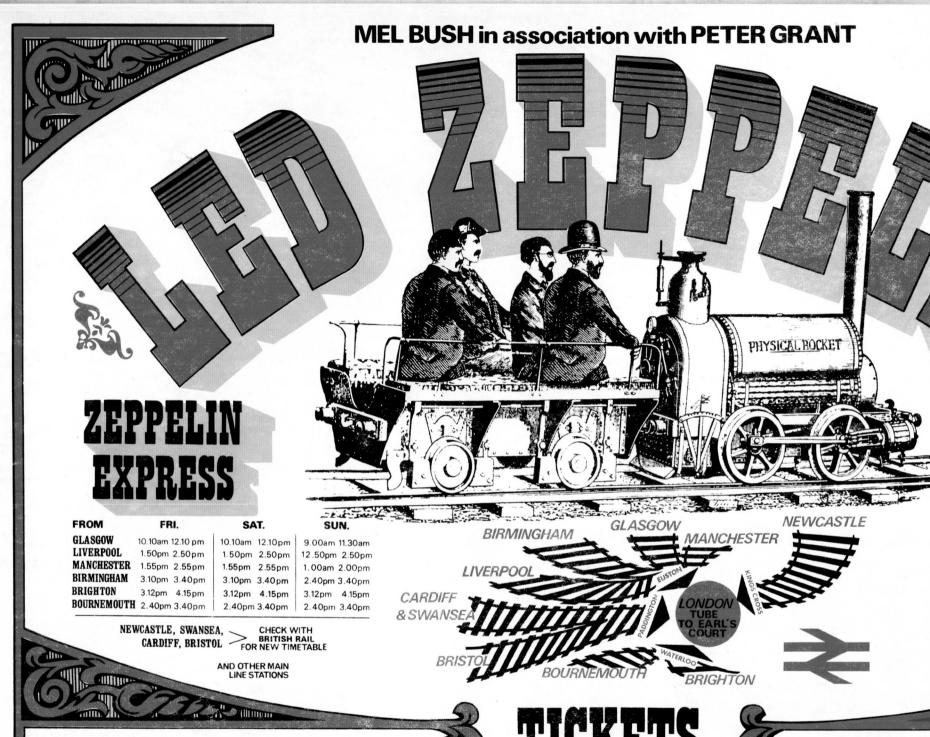

EARL'S
COURT

SAT SUN
24th 25th

Y at 8p.m.

s open
p.m.

"1974 DIDN'T REALLY HAPPEN. 1975 WILL BE MUCH BETTER."

Jimmy Page

LEFT: Led Zeppelin played five legendary nights at London's Earl's Court in May 1975. The stylish poster played on the theme of arriving by train. Footage from the concerts was released on DVD 20 years later.

JOHN BONHAM

"Bonzo" was the heart and soul of Led Zeppelin. The Bonham sound, purposeful and commanding, was woven into their creative fabric. Many numbers were built around the drum and guitar riffs he and Page worked out together, such as 'Immigrant Song', 'Black Dog' and 'When The Levee Breaks'. His sense of swing came from his jazz and blues roots, and it was Bonham's clever use of cymbals and percussion that brought such drama to 'Dazed And Confused' and 'Whole Lotta Love'.

LEFT: Bonzo strikes an unusually thoughtful pose.

ABOVE: John Henry Bonham – the hardest, heaviest and loudest drummer in rock music.

Page knew how to utilize Bonham's power to full effect in the studio. He would hold the drums back until they could make a grand entrance, most effectively on 'Stairway To Heaven'. All the key albums featured earth-shaking moments from Bonham, including his introduction to 'Rock And Roll', the thunder unleashed on 'Kashmir' and that most sampled of Zeppelin tracks, 'When The Levee Breaks'.

In an era when drummers became celebrities, Bonham stood out. His extended solos became a feature of concerts, as much part of the Zeppelin image as Page waving his violin bow or Plant's mighty screams.

John Henry Bonham was born in Redditch, Worcestershire, on May 31, 1948. Father Jack was a carpenter with his own building firm; mum Joan ran a newsagent's shop. John and brother Michael went to Wilton House private school until John was 11, when he moved to Lodge Farm Secondary Modern School.

When John left school at 16 it was assumed he would go into the family business, and he often laboured on building sites, but as he said later, "Drumming was the only thing I was any good at and I stuck at it." At five, he'd begun hammering on pots and pans and used a handy bath salts container with wires across the bottom to give the effect of a snare drum. His father took him to see American drummer Sonny Payne with the Harry James Orchestra and he was mesmerized by Payne's soloing; Gene Krupa's drumming on 'Sing, Sing' Sing' in the movie *The Benny Goodman Story* was another source of inspiration.

His father bought him a proper kit when he was 15: "It was almost prehistoric. Most of it was rust, but I was determined to be a drummer as soon as I left school."

His first semi-professional group, Terry Webb and the Spiders, dressed as Teddy Boys and played rock 'n' roll. After a year, he joined A Way of Life and, aged 17, married girlfriend Pat. Although he occasionally had to return to building sites to earn a living, he carried on playing and worked with singer Nicky James. "I was so keen to play when I quit school I'd have played for nothing. I did for a long time but my parents stuck by me. I never had any lessons and just played the way I wanted. They used to say I was too loud and there was no future in playing that

way." One exasperated recording engineer told Bonham he was "unrecordable" and ought to play quieter. It was the drummer's great delight some years later to send him a gold Led Zeppelin album inscribed to John Bonham, with a note saying, "Thanks for the advice."

He had promised his wife he'd give up drumming, but couldn't resist getting behind a kit. He'd played with Steve Brett and the Mavericks before joining the Crawling King Snakes, where he met Plant. John found a well-paid gig touring with Tim Rose, the American singer who recorded 'Hey Joe' before Jimi Hendrix. When Robert excitedly called him about a possible gig with The New Yardbirds, he wasn't interested.

Bonham had developed a reputation for his technique, which drew on influences from Sonny Payne to Buddy Rich and from Joe Morello to Carmine Appice of Vanilla Fudge; Appice's speed with a bass drum pedal particularly intrigued Bonham, who would develop his own powerful foot action.

Page had thought about recruiting B J Wilson of Procol Harum and also contacted Aynsley Dunbar, who had worked with John Mayall's Bluesbreakers. When Aynsley joined Frank Zappa, Plant told Page about Bonham, explaining he was the loudest and heaviest drummer in the country and would be ideal.

Jimmy went to The Marquee to see Bonzo backing Tim Rose. He later called Grant in the States to report: "This guy plays so good and so loud we must get him. He plays so loud promoters won't rebook him!"

When Grant returned to London he discovered Bonham didn't have a working telephone. He sent a succession of telegrams which the drummer ignored, thinking The New Yardbirds sounded like a cabaret act, akin to the New Vaudeville Band.

Eventually John succumbed to pressure and came to London for the first rehearsal in Soho. He played well, but when Jimmy asked him to simplify the beat he carried on regardless. Page was visibly annoyed, and when Grant saw this he asked Bonham, "Do you like your job in the band? If so, do as this man says or f**k off. Behave yourself, Bonham, or you'll disappear, through different doors."

Once the ground rules were established, Bonham became a loyal and integral part of Led Zeppelin. His famed drum solo, dubbed 'Moby Dick', appeared on *Led Zeppelin II* and a live version on 1976's soundtrack album *The Song Remains The Same*. An unusual electronic drum solo, 'Bonzo's Montreux', appeared on the posthumous *Coda* album in 1982.

When Led Zeppelin became a mega-group John was happy to spend his pay on cars and property and become a gentleman farmer, but his greatest delight was being able to support his family and encourage son Jason, who would later became a top drummer in his own right, even playing with the revived Led Zeppelin.

The band embarked on a European tour in 1980. Although unwell, Bonham completed most of the dates, but died on September 25, 1980, after rehearsing at Page's house in Windsor prior to a planned US tour. Led Zeppelin died with him, but his drums roar on in the band's legacy.

LEFT: Unusual in the rock world, Bonham made extensive use of orchestral timpani.

BELOW: Bonzo dons bowler and white jumpsuit for the legendary Madison Square Garden gigs in 1975.

1976

The premiere of the long-awaited Led Zeppelin film *The Song Remains The Same* was a highlight of a year when the group once more made their presence felt around the world. Even while *Physical Graffiti* was echoing across the airwaves, the band came up with a new album, but they avoided live appearances during 1976. Cinemas became the only venues where fans could get their fix.

In Paris for New Year, Plant took his first steps since the crash five months earlier, joking: "One small step for man, one giant leap for six nights at Madison Square Garden."

While Page worked on mixing the movie soundtrack, Plant was pressed into doing interviews to discuss their forthcoming album. In February Led Zeppelin won many of the categories in the *New Musical Express* annual readers' poll. The following month Page returned to London from New York and did his share of interviews, set up at the Swan Song offices in Fulham.

Then on April 6 the seventh Led Zeppelin album, *Presence*, was released. Recorded in Munich, it featured seven tracks, with 'Achilles' Last Stand' considered among the best. Robert described it as "full of energy because of that sort of primeval fight within me, to get back and to get better. There's a lot of determination on the album, and fist-banging on the table."

Presence got mixed reviews but went straight to Number One in the UK charts and topped the US charts a week later. The full track list included 'Achilles' Last Stand', 'For Your Life', 'Royal Orleans', 'Nobody's Fault But Mine', 'Candy Store Rock', 'Hots On For Nowhere' and 'Tea For One'.

Although the group had cancelled all their tour dates following Robert's injury, he was able to put in an appearance on stage, jamming alongside Page at a Bad Company gig at the Los Angeles Forum on May 23. Later that month rumours spread that the

ABOVE: New look. John Paul Jones claimed to change his appearance to enable him to pass unrecognized in public while on tour.

LEFT: Messrs Plant, Page and Grant get smart for the premiere of *The Song Remains The Same*.

ABOVE: Led Zeppelin "In Concert And Beyond" – so ran the posters for the movie *The Song Remains The Same*.

ABOVE: The band at the opening of what Peter Grant called: "The most expensive home movie ever made".

whole band might appear at London's Marquee Club but in the event only Jones turned up to sit in with The Pretty Things.

In July anxious promoters hoped the band would put on a one-off show at Wembley Stadium. Whereas most artists would fall on their knees at such an offer, Zeppelin declined. They were too busy preparing their movie, and in any case Plant wasn't ready for a strenuous stage performance. He did attend a rock festival in Cardiff, and shortly afterwards Dave Edmunds was signed to Swan Song.

During September Page produced a percussion track featuring Bonham that would eventually surface as 'Bonzo's Montreux' on the 1982 album *Coda*. In October TV viewers got a rare glimpse of the band on the small screen when BBC 2's *Old Grey Whistle Test* showed a clip from *The Song Remains The Same*.

On October 20 the film premiered at Cinema One in Manhattan, New York. A special quadraphonic sound system hired from Showco was installed in the theatre; powerful hi-fi sound was vital for the film's success. All the band members attended, with the $25,000 proceeds going to a children's charity. On October 22 the double soundtrack album was released simultaneously worldwide and the film was also given its West Coast premiere in Los Angeles.

The film Peter Clifton finally achieved managed to blend the famed fantasy sequences depicting the band members' personalities, backstage scenes and live footage shot at Madison Square Garden in 1973. Some scenes had been reshot at Shepperton Studios to help match the soundtrack and the footage.

Bonham's appearance driving a drag-racing car drew cheers from the crowd at the London premiere. The other sequences, such as Page climbing the mountain near Boleskin House and Jones as a night-rider, were greeted with some bemusement.

Some thought the star of the film was manager Grant, whose ferocity berating a concert promoter backstage in Baltimore in 1973 lit up the screen. In a towering rage, he was complaining about a pirate merchandiser being allowed to trade within the venue in order to profit from Zeppelin's show. The robbery at the Drake Hotel in New York also provided another dramatic episode when newsreel footage was acquired of Peter being arrested for assaulting a photographer at a press conference.

As a result of this candour, not all the reviews were complimentary. Dave Marsh in *Rolling Stone* said the film was "a tribute to their rapaciousness and inconsideration … their sense of themselves merits only contempt." However, Chris Charlesworth in *Melody Maker* branded it a "classy, and surely enormously

successful film." It grossed $200,000 in the first week of release and the soundtrack album went platinum and topped the charts. Page thought the film provided a good record of the band's past work and Grant later conceded: "Some of it was OK: but what did we know about making films? I did enjoy the premieres and meeting all the media folk. It was the most expensive home movie ever made."

On October 30 Led Zeppelin gave the news all their fans had been awaiting. With the movie safely out of the way, the band would return to live performances with a world tour due to start in America in February 1977.

Meanwhile a double European premiere was staged in two West End cinemas on November 4, followed by a jolly party at the Floral Hall, Covent Garden, attended by Robert Plant. A couple of days later *The Song Remains The Same* was screened in Birmingham, Glasgow, Liverpool, Cambridge, Leeds, Reading and Southampton.

Led Zeppelin were harnessing the power of film and rock in a pioneering form, although the Woodstock documentary had already shown how mixed media could succeed. There was no doubt Led Zeppelin were happiest doing what they did best, and so they began rehearsing in London for their 1977 tour, kicking off with their hot new song 'Achilles' Last Stand'. They were ready for action but, once again, the fates would conspire against them.

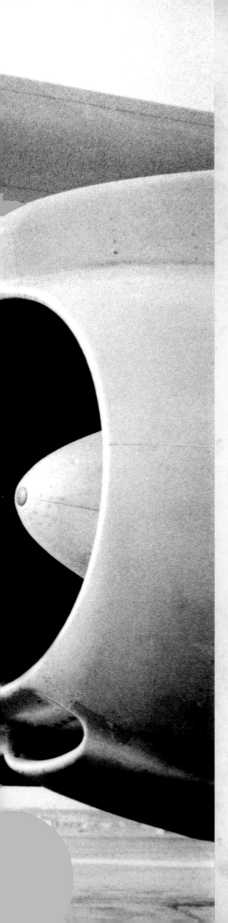

"ONCE I HAD ALL THE TIME IN THE WORLD AND NO MONEY. NOW I HAVE THE MONEY BUT NO TIME."

John Paul Jones

LEFT: The private jet – at the time *de rigeur* for any self-respecting rock gods.

PRESENCE

It was the album that nearly didn't happen. Injuries Plant suffered in that crash in 1975 put him out of action. With a broken ankle and elbow, he was advised he wouldn't be able to walk for months, and recording and touring seemed out of the question but by the end of the year Plant was well enough for the band to contemplate work on a new album. Led Zeppelin met at Musicland Studios in Germany. It was the first time they had chosen a European studio and the fresh location seemed to encourage them.

LED ZEPPELIN
PRESENCE

ACHILLES LAST STAND
FOR YOUR LIFE
ROYAL ORLEANS
NOBODYS FAULT BUT MINE
CANDY STORE ROCK
HOTS ON FOR NOWHERE
TEA FOR ONE

SS 8416

The stand-out track on *Presence* is undoubtedly 'Achilles' Last Stand', a magnificent performance by any band's standards. Taken at a galloping pace, the dramatic theme summons images of warriors on trusty steeds charging through forests and across the battlefields of myth and legend. It's hard to believe Plant sang this while on crutches; perhaps even in a wheelchair. Some might have felt that in creating his own Zeppelin saga he was empathizing with Achilles, hero of Homer's *Iliad*, who was mortally wounded by an arrow that flew into his heel. However, Robert declared the lyrics were inspired by the view from the top of the Atlas Mountains.

Excited by the roar of the band during the recording session, Robert had another accident he feared would endanger his recovery. Running towards the vocal booth with the aid of a crutch, he fell heavily on his injured foot and suffered spasms of extreme pain. Plant, who was rushed to hospital, feared he'd re-opened the fracture and would never be able to walk again, but mercifully this hadn't happened and he carried on working with the aid of painkillers.

The glittering steely guitar overdubs unleashed during 'Achilles' Last Stand' clash like swords, except Page's weapon of choice was a Gibson Les Paul bonded to a trusty Marshall amplifier. An intensely powerful arrangement, it explored different movements in typical Zeppelin fashion. The song became a concert staple, taking its place alongside 'Kashmir' as a new classic.

After this, the rest of the album seemed of an anticlimax to some, but there were plenty of nuggets meriting closer study, and just as rewarding in more subtle ways. 'For Your Life' examines aspects of the rock life style they had all experienced and Robert found dissatisfying; he later described it as an admonition of those who fell into the trap of the LA drugs and groupie scene.

The next song, 'Royal Orleans', is another reflection on the strangeness of rock stars' lives, a tale of someone waking up in bed with a drag queen at a hotel in the French quarter of New Orleans. This "someone" was quite close to the band and it is further alleged the unlikely couple set the bed alight with a cigarette and the fire brigade had to be called.

'Nobody's Fault But Mine' is full of long pauses during the narrative and has strong harmonica-playing from Plant, the blues aficionado. The number develops from hesitant beginnings and is said to have been inspired by a 1920s Blind Willie Johnson blues.

Rock 'n' roller 'Candy Store Rock' harks back to the days when Teddy Boys ruled the UK youth scene. Bonham is in his element, driving the beat, while Robert improvises the lyrics from the dimly-remembered Elvis records of his youth. It was released as a single in America in June 1976, backed with 'Royal Orleans'.

'Hots On For Nowhere' was devised in the studio and is a curious mixture of childlike innocence and seething bitterness, with its dancing beat and biting lyrics. Bonham plays with undiminished fire and Page offers a guitar break of dazzling dexterity. Its driving simplicity sets up the listener for the album's final track.

'Tea For One' is a beautiful song about pain and loneliness. Following an anguished guitar introduction it becomes a ballad that's both tasteful and sombre, Page's extended guitar solo being described by Plant as "brilliant". The title came from a period during a US tour when Robert was feeling especially homesick and found himself sitting in a hotel room drinking "tea for one." Whatever moods the band members were enduring during difficult times, they hadn't lost their ability to lose themselves in the joy of making music for their own satisfaction.

The album was released in America on March 31, 1976, and in Britain on April 6, in a white sleeve designed by the Hipgnosis team, famed for Pink Floyd's *Dark Side Of The Moon*. Unlike *Physical Graffiti* there was no band name or album title on the front, although they did appear along the spine. Some albums ended up being stickered! Aubrey Powell of Hipgnosis suggested the title, sensing a "presence" surrounding the band.

The cover photographs depict all-American stereotypes contemplating a mysterious twisted piece of metal known as "The Object", partly inspired by the iconic "obelisk" featured in Stanley Kubrick's movie *2001: A Space Odyssey*. As one point the album was to be called *Obelisk*, though Plant preferred *Thanksgiving* to express his relief at completing the task. However, *Presence* was Page's final choice.

Huge advance orders ensured it went gold immediately and was Number 1 in the UK and US charts within weeks. Page later said he thought *Presence* was an under-rated album and their best in terms of emotional content: yet it was it was all done in three weeks. Many bands could take as many months, years even, to finish an album.

Under deadline pressure, Page explained, they had cut all the frills, such as acoustic numbers and keyboard arrangements, and concentrated on the core of guitar riffs and vocals backed by bass and drums, spending up to 18 hours a day in the studio trying to get it all done. The best news for Plant after finishing *Presence* was that he could walk unaided and make his true presence felt on stage again.

BELOW. With his injuries now behind him, Robert Plant was once again able to take to the stage.

"IF HE DOESN'T STAY HEALTHY, I'LL KILL HIM!"

Robert Plant remains concerned about Page's health as they begin yet another world tour in 1977.

LEFT: The band's concert movie *The Song Remains the Same*, enjoys a premiere at the glitzy Fox Wilshire Theater, Los Angeles, October 21 1976.

TOP: Advertising flyer for the Led Zeppelin movie, 1977

BOTTOM: A ticket for the premier of *The Song Remains the Same*, 1976.

RIGHT: The Object (as seen on the cover of *Presence*), 1976.

1977

After ten years of astounding success it seemed the band was destined to go on for ever. Then in 1977 a string of disasters threatened to put an end to everything. In fact they would carry on for three more years but 1977 was not the happiest of times for Led Zeppelin.

ABOVE: Luthier Andy Manson built this mandolin/six-/12-string acoustic combo for John Paul Jones.

RIGHT: Jimmy Page puts his feet up and prepares for some relaxed listening at home.

FAR RIGHT: Rock dinosaur? Still nobody could swagger on stage quite like Robert Plant.

The year began with the promise of a world tour, to begin in the US on February 27. During January they began rehearsals at Manticore, a converted cinema in Fulham owned by rival supergroup Emerson, Lake and Palmer.

Punk rock was emerging; while many long-established groups felt threatened by aggressive new bands such as the Sex Pistols, who called them "dinosaurs", Led Zeppelin welcomed the trend towards anarchism. Plant and Page went to see The Damned at The Roxy in Covent Garden and announced they'd enjoyed the show, and Bonham and Plant saw Generation X, Eater and The Damned there. Maybe it was the foetid atmosphere at punk gigs, but Robert contracted tonsillitis and their 11th US tour had to be postponed. The dates were rescheduled and eventually they opened in Dallas on April 1. Fifty-one concerts awaited, in

30 cities, and a million fans, cigarette lighters poised ready to hold aloft during 'Stairway To Heaven'. They would be playing for three hours a night, something which amazed recent convert George Harrison; The Beatles, he said, never played live for more than about 30 minutes. Video projector screens were set up at the biggest venues and Showco provided massive PA systems. Tickets sold at a rate of 72,000 a day.

Page seemed to take all the hard work in his stride, having recovered from the illness that had affected him on previous tours. It was reported he was taking a daily mixture of bananas and protein for strength. Said Plant: "We've got a new Jimmy Page and he's the leader again. If he doesn't stay healthy, I'll kill him!"

In May, about halfway through the tour they took a 17-day break; Page flew to Egypt to visit the pyramids. The others, plus Grant, went to London to receive an Ivor Novello Award on May 12 for their contribution to music. The tour resumed on May 18 in Birmingham, Alabama. At many shows there were riots and arrests as fans without tickets tried to get in. Some of the worst violence was at Tampa Stadium, Florida, on June 3 when 20 minutes in, during *The Song Remains The Same*, lightning tore through the sky and the heavens opened. As rain was pouring on to the stage, the road crew feared the danger of electrocution. Robert told the crowd: "We have to stop or our equipment will blow up!" When there was crowd unrest police in riot gear arrived and began bashing heads. More than 100 fans were injured and the Mayor announced Led Zeppelin would be forever banned from Tampa to protect its citizens. A replacement show the following day was cancelled.

They played six nights at Madison Square Garden, New York, between June 7 and 14, and between June 21 and 27 slotted in another six at the Forum, Los Angeles. On June 28 they flew home for a rest, returning to the States on July 17 to play the Kingdome, Seattle. All seemed well; then on July 23 a violent

scene developed backstage at a concert at the Coliseum in Oakland. Grant, tour manager Cole, Bonham and security man John Bindon were involved in a clash with promoter Bill Graham's own team, attacking a security man when he refused to let Grant's son Warren take a nameplate from a dressing-room door as a souvenir. The guard was hospitalized; Cole, Bonham, Bindon and Grant were arrested and charged with assault. A civil action followed, demanding $2 million in damages.

The following day the band flew to New Orleans for a date at the Superdome on July 30. However, on the day they arrived news came from England that Robert's son Karac had been taken ill with an infection. The next day he was worse, and was taken to hospital, but was dead on arrival. Robert immediately flew home and the rest of the tour was cancelled.

There was more talk of a split in September, but in London Page conducted several interviews to quash the rumours, angry at suggestions they were under some sort of "curse." However, the future looked uncertain, and in the event Zeppelin would never return to the States in their original form. They left behind a lot of bad feeling, and *Rolling Stone* magazine's headline read: "The wrong goodbye: Led Zeppelin leaves America."

LEFT: Page used his EDS-1275 guitar on 'Stairway To Heaven' – the climax of Zeppelin's set.

BELOW: The 1977 US tour may have broken box-office records but it would all soon end in tears.

Despite this nutritious diet, during one of four nights at the Chicago Stadium Page had to sit down while soloing on 'Ten Years Gone' and an hour in, the band was forced to stop. Page was taken back to his hotel, said to be suffering from food poisoning. "The pain was unbearable" he said later. "It was the first time we had to stop a gig like that. We always have a go because we're not a rip-off band." He insisted they were enjoying themselves on the road and rebutted rumours of an impending split: "It's a stag party that never ends, and it's great to be back on the road after all the trials and tribulations of the past year. It's great to see the smiles. This is no last tour. We're here and we'll always come back. It'd be a criminal act to break up this band."

Zeppelin broke the record set at Tampa in 1973 when they played to 76,229 fans at the Pontiac Silverdome on April 30, earning them and the promoter $800,000. The hotel wrecking sprees continued, with Plant's room at the Ambassador East Hotel in Chicago a particular target. He paid for any damage, however, insisting it was not done out of boredom or "road fever" – but just for fun.

"THERE IS NO QUESTION OF SPLITTING UP."

Jimmy Page

1978

'Ten Years Gone', a song from *Physical Graffiti*, mused on the tricks of fate and destiny. The phrase returned to haunt Led Zeppelin in their tenth year together, as they pondered on the events that had blighted their otherwise glittering success story. They might have wanted to forget 1977, but it could not be entirely shaken off as they contemplated their future.

It was many months before Plant would recover from the shock of his son's death and he spent all his time at home with his family. Page spent his time writing songs and going through the vast mountain of tapes the band had accumulated over the years. He proposed using live material for an album that would put excerpts from concerts in chronological order. These would include shows at venues such as the Royal Albert Hall in 1969, Southampton University in 1971 and Earls Court in 1975. It would provide an official record of Zeppelin's growth as opposed to the many bootleg LPs then circulating among record collectors: but it wasn't until the CD era that officially-sanctioned Zeppelin compilations began to appear.

Meanwhile Bonham and Jones also spent their days at home with their families, perhaps coming to terms with what had happened in California and trying to escape from the rock 'n' roll lifestyle.

Page was the only band member who felt able to conduct interviews during this crisis period and confirmed: "There's no question of splitting up. I know Robert wants to work again and he'll start working at his own pace."

On February 16, 1978, the criminal cases against Grant, Bonham, Cole and Bindon were heard in California and all received suspended prison sentences and fines. None of the men appeared in court.

It wasn't until May that the band reunited in somewhat chastened mood at Clearwell Castle in the Forest of Dean to rehearse and make plans. By the summer rumours began to spread that Led Zeppelin might perform in the UK, but these proved unfounded.

Instead, Plant cheered himself up by singing with various bands of old mates in his former stamping-ground in the Black Country.

Having spent the early part of the year quietly with his family, Plant reappeared at Wolverley Memorial Hall in July, singing with an outfit entitled Melvin Giganticus

ABOVE: Robert Plant namechecks US all-girl rockers, The Runaways – the band from which Joan Jett would later emerge.

LEFT: Page thought a live compilation would album lessen the impact of the bootleggers, who plagued Zeppelin with their illegal releases.

LEFT: Jimmy Page brandishes his Les Paul once more.

ABOVE: The new tour dates were met with excitement. Nobody – least of all the band – thought it would be their last.

and the Turd Burglars. His choice of songs included rousing versions of 'I Gotta Woman' and 'Blue Suede Shoes'. The following month he sang along with pub rockers Dr. Feelgood at Club Amnesia in Ibiza. Atlantic executive Phil Carson sat in on bass guitar, reviving memories of his jams with Zeppelin in happier times. The club's manager Stu Lyons said later: "Robert looked in great shape and sounded fantastic."

On September 15 there was a Zeppelin "family" event when tour manager Cole got married, and the Fulham ceremony was attended by Page, Plant and Jones. The next day Plant joined Swan Song artist Dave Edmunds for his encore number at Birmingham Odeon. There was more music-making when Jones and Bonham were invited to participate in a recording session with Paul McCartney's Rockestra at Abbey Road Studios, to lay down tracks for the Wings album *Back To The Egg*.

In October Led Zeppelin got back to work and began rehearsals in London for a projected new album, but for tax reasons they had to get out of the country for a while and flew to Stockholm on November 6 to make the album which was to be called *In Through The Out Door* at Abba's Polar Music studio.

Robert explained that Abba had invited them to come to Sweden to try out the studios. Normally they would have gone to Los Angeles in order to soak up the vibes and get into heavy rock mode. "To trek to Sweden in the middle of winter, the studio had to be good and it was. It was sensational and had just the live sound that we like."

Once the recordings were completed Jimmy Page began mixing the material at his home studio in Plumpton over the Christmas holiday. The year had flashed by, and for their fans around the world it seemed a deathly silence had fallen over the band. They feared they'd never hear 'Whole Lotta Love', 'Kashmir' and 'Stairway To Heaven' live again; but their patience was rewarded and anxiety allayed. Soon the announcements came in the music press. Led Zeppelin was staying together and did have plans for the future. 1979 would provide a reprieve for the band and they would be back on stage one more time with a show in the UK intended as a celebration: but in another twist of fate, it would prove to be their swansong.

1979

Despite the traumas and tragedy, it seemed inconceivable the world's greatest band should be allowed to fade away. Page was determined to keep Zeppelin airborne and with Grant – under orders to lose weight after stress-related heart trouble – made plans to restore the group to flying condition.

The year began with good news; the birth of Robert and Maureen's son Logan on January 21. Understandably, Plant wanted to spend time at home, but in February the band returned to Stockholm to continue mixing the album. There was even talk of a European tour, but instead, they spent time catching up on the simple pleasures they had missed during Zeppelin's early years; Jones and Plant went to Dave Edmunds' wedding reception on May 8. Then on May 22 it was announced they would headline a show at Knebworth, Hertfordshire, promoted by Fred Bannister, creator of the Bath Festivals. It would coincide with the release of their eighth studio album, *In Through The Out Door*. They opted for a showcase rather than another tour

because, as Grant exclaimed: "We didn't want to start all over again. We're the biggest band in the world, so we'll go out there and show them we still are." Names being mentioned for the Knebworth bill included Dire Straits, Fairport Convention, Joni Mitchell, Little Feat, Bob Seger, Van Morrison, the Boomtown Rats, B B King, Aerosmith and the Marshall Tucker Band, though few of these were eventually booked. On June 9 Plant gave a BBC Radio 1 interview, his first in two years. Then on July 4 it was announced there would be another show at Knebworth, due to such huge demand. Zeppelin rehearsed at Bray Studios, and on July 19 it was confirmed that The New Barbarians, led by Rolling

BELOW: A superbly colourful Japanese poster for *The Song Remains The Same*.

ABOVE: Robert Plant with daughter Carmen. She would later marry Charlie Jones, Plant's bass player throughout the 1990s.

BELOW: Page used cheap Danelectro guitars with altered tunings on such notable tracks as 'Kashmir' and 'Black Mountain Side'.

ABOVE: More than just a four-string man, John Paul Jones displays some delicate fretwork during an acoustic session.

Stones Keith Richards and Ronnie Wood, would support them at the second event.

To warm up, Zeppelin went back to their roots with shows at the Falkoner Theatre, Copenhagen, on July 23 and 24; they first played in the city in September 1968.

On August 3 they arrived at Knebworth to soundcheck and the following day took the stage supported by Fairport Convention, Commander Cody, Chas and Dave, Southside Johnny and the Asbury Jukes and Todd Rundgren's Utopia. Zeppelin played for three hours and did four encores. It was their first UK gig since 1975 and their first anywhere since July 1977. Showco installed a 100,000W PA, a 600,000W light show and a vast video screen.

At the second show on August 11 the line-up was almost identical, Keith Richards and The New Barbarians replacing Fairport. Both they and Zeppelin kept fans waiting, which didn't help the atmosphere. There was some debate about numbers, but Grant arranged a helicopter to photograph the crowd and sent the pictures to NASA, who reported there were 210,000 at the first show and 180,000 at the second.

Some reviews were brutal. As the decade ended, "new" sounds and fashions – punk, New Wave, New Romanticism, New Heavy Metal – were being touted to replace the supergroups. A new generation of critics saw Zeppelin as representing the "dinosaur" breed of despised stadium rockers,

and were emboldened by the perceived loss of power and prestige they had suffered in America. One review of *In Through The Out Door*, released on August 20, called it "A Whole Lotta Bluff". *Rolling Stone* magazine at one point referred to "Sad Zep" and one Sunday newspaper described the band appearing at Knebworth as "the worst and noisiest group in the history of rock music". Another scribe said they had "squeezed their lemons dry a long time ago."

Not everyone hated them. *Musicians Only* stated: "In view of the excessive tripe written about Led Zeppelin at Knebworth it is a matter of urgency that fans who could not be present should be reassured. The band was excellent, their performance superb. The cacophony of orchestrated criticism which followed their appearance was laughable." Even so, the young Knebworth audience hadn't reacted as exuberantly as in the past, perhaps exhausted by the long wait for the New Barbarians and the lacklustre performance that followed; even Grant conceded they had been "rusty". It took Led Zeppelin at full blast to restore their enthusiasm, having been stuck in a field for long hours. At times it was possible to hear a pin drop as 100,000 stood in the darkness, craning to see the remote figures on stage or focus on the screens. Zeppelin performed 'Stairway To Heaven', 'No Quarter' and 'Trampled Underfoot', Jones showcased on piano as strongly as Page on guitar. Plant's voice had lost none of its spine-tingling vibrancy and was especially effective on slow blues. Bonham cut out his 'Moby Dick' solo but had all his old power; if anything, the band seemed even tighter and more cohesive. Despite some misgivings, Knebworth augured well for a creative future.

Though the press were taking swipes at what seemed like every possible opportunity, the group's fans remained loyal. Despite punk's supposed dominance, Zeppelin won most of the categories in the *Melody Maker* Annual Readers' Poll. Plant, Jones, Bonham and Grant attended the reception at the Waldorf Astoria on November 28 to collect seven awards. The much-derided *In Through The Out Door* rocketed up the charts and by the end of September had sold three million, remaining Number One in the US for seven weeks. Zeppelin's entire catalogue also appeared in *Billboard*'s Top 200 album chart, a feat no other artists had achieved.

In the run-up to Christmas the band allowed themselves the fun of attending other artists' gigs, including a trip to Wembley to see Abba in action. Page went to see Paul McCartney and Wings in Brighton, and Paul and Linda McCartney, with Denny Laine, came to visit him at Plumpton. Zeppelin's comeback year ended when Plant, Jones and Bonham went to see Wings at the Hammersmith Odeon and joined McCartney on stage for a grand finale performed by his Rockestra ensemble.

They had survived to fight another day. Now Led Zeppelin faced a new decade, determined to reclaim their crown as the world's greatest group.

IN THROUGH THE OUT DOOR

Led Zeppelin's eighth and final studio album was the band's last creative act together before the tragic, final meltdown took place.

They could have called it *The Last Chance Saloon*, if only because of the enigmatic album cover. It depicts a lonely man in a white hat and suit, sitting in a honky-tonk bar observed by various other characters including a pianist and bar-keeper. There were six different versions of the sleeve to entice collectors, but once again there was no mention of the band's name or album title. As with *Presence*, the relevant information could only be found printed in minute lettering on the spine.

In Through The Out Door opened up a turbulent stage in their career, when they faced the challenges of a new musical era. Disco, punk and electronic innovations were in the air. Zeppelin needed to bid farewell to the 1970s, but carried considerable baggage both musically and in terms of their history. On their eighth album they appeared determined to come up with interesting concepts worthy of their heritage. They seemed very keen to embrace new and different styles, while keeping faith with their rock 'n' roll roots.

Two and a half years had elapsed since *Presence*. They convened at Abba's Polar Studio in Stockholm at the invitation of the famed vocal group, who wanted them to experience the hi-tech facilities available. The British lads were assisted by Swedish engineers Leif Mases and Lennart Ostlund. The new album was eventually released in August 1979 and first impressions revealed a sharper, brighter, Nordic sound had been achieved. The band itself sounded different: tighter, less ramshackle and a tad more sophisticated.

Many of the songs evoked an introspective mood, but there were joyful moments and brash new rhythms that John Bonham in particular seemed to relish. 'In The Evening', the first of seven diverse tracks, begins with a cascade of guitar effects. An insistent theme performed with a stomping beat tends to swamp Robert Plant's vocals.

Only the cry of "I need your love" emerges from the clamour of hammered strings. Page uses a Gizmotron, the guitar effects device invented by Lol Creme and Kevin Godley of 10cc, to enhance distortion, and this complements the song's message about distorted values. As Plant points out: "It's lonely at the bottom and it's dizzy at the top."

'South Bound Saurez' has a choppy piano motif devised by John Paul Jones, and an angry, buzzing guitar solo peps up this old-time rock 'n' roll revival with New Orleans roots.

The track 'Fool In the Rain' has some nifty and precise drumming from Bonham that shows how he was capable of playing so much more than a heavy backbeat. Robert sings in relaxed mode and is more effective than when screaming against the band. A samba rhythm pervades a song that would reach Number 21 in the *Billboard* singles chart in January 1980 but was never played live.

'Hot Dog' is close in spirit to Shakin' Stevens or even Bill Wyman's Rhythm Kings in its joyful celebration of Fifties rockabilly. Robert is in his element, warbling through tricky lyrics about seeking a fetching Texan gal who takes off on a Greyhound bus. The band sound like they're whooping it up in the bar depicted on the album cover. The number was dedicated to Zeppelin's trusty Texan Showco road crew and was filmed for a promotional video.

'Carouselambra' is the biggest surprise. While not in quite the same league as 'Achilles' Last Stand' or 'Kashmir', this team effort still produces exhilarating results. Confident and thrusting, 'Carouselambra' is powered by storming drums and organ riffs that hark back to the Stax sound of the Sixties.

During this ten-minute epic an unexpected change in mood sees the tempo dip as Page unleashes chiming, mysterious chords, casting a riveting, hypnotic spell. The lyrics are largely unfathomable but have a mystical origin and are aimed at a specific person for whom all will one day be revealed. As the song picks up the pace once more cataclysmic drum fills round off one of Zeppelin's most under-rated works.

'All My Love' is the penultimate number and is basically a pop song written by Plant and Jones, utilizing a synthesizer rather more than the guitar. It seems like the sort of material the senior members of the band might have played in their session days, and is far removed from the usual Zeppelin style.

'I'm Gonna Crawl' rounds off the album with a heartfelt performance. Delivered by Robert with all the passion of an Otis Redding or James Brown, it's complemented by a fine guitar solo from Jimmy. Given the sad mood that prevails as 'I'm Gonna Crawl' fades away into silence, Zeppelin's last stand is all the more poignant.

In Through The Out Door sold some four millions copies in America and topped the US and UK charts, showing that the punk rock craze had no effect on Led Zeppelin's ability to generate massive sales. Jimmy Page had wanted the band to experiment during the making of this album. The music they produced pointed towards an intriguing but unknowable future.

LEFT: (left to right) Peter Grant, Robert Plant and John Paul Jones chew the fat over a few drinks and a smoke.

ABOVE: The band may have been through some tough times but a Led Zeppelin gig was still a high energy occasion.

TOP: Led Zeppelin had always been beset by rumours of a split … which were laughed off by Plant and Page.

1980+

Ultimately, Knebworth had been a triumph. As the new decade dawned it seemed the band was ready to take its place as a creative force once more, but there was still a lot of work to be done and Plant's guarded comment after their concerts was: "It's been quite good."

Their return was greeted with delight by a music industry hit by an unexpected slump in US sales. With a dearth of new acts, only they could be relied on to get buyers back into stores. *In Through The Out Door* sold millions and was their seventh album to enter the charts at Number One in its first week. In America Swan Song issued a single version of 'Fool In The Rain' coupled with 'Hot Dog' just before Christmas 1979. It was a Top 20 hit. Zeppelin's magic was working again.

In April 1980 a European tour was announced and rehearsals began at the Rainbow Theatre, London on April 27, later moving to the New Victoria theatre. The tour was expected to start in May but some dates had to be altered and it eventually kicked off in June. More rehearsals were held at Shepperton Studios, indicating a need to get into shape after their long lay-off. The band claimed they disliked rehearsing and preferred playing to an audience, but they needed to tighten up arrangements and revise the vast amount of material accumulated over the previous decade.

After Page completed the purchase of actor Michael Caine's former home in Windsor for £900,000 on June 17, the "Over Europe 80" tour began at the Westfalen Halle, Dortmund, Germany, followed by Cologne (18), Brussels (20), Rotterdam (21), Bremen (23), Hanover (24), Vienna (26) and Nuremberg (27), where the show ended after only three numbers with Bonham's collapse from exhaustion. Wrapped in a red blanket, strapped into an ambulance and given a handbell for emergency use, he asked his manager how he looked; Grant replied, "Like Father Christmas!"

Bonham recovered in time for the rest of the tour, and shows in Zurich (29), Frankfurt (30), Mannheim (July 2 and 3), Munich (5) and Berlin (7). In Munich Bonham invited his old friend Simon Kirke, drummer with Bad Company, to sit in; they set up two drum kits and played together on 'Whole Lotta Love.' Kirke had to learn the arrangement in the hotel just before the gig, with John slapping the drum parts on his knees. It would be the last time he saw his old friend. After the tour Bonham summed up: "It was a bit of a gamble but it's worked really well. We want to keep working. There's lots of possibilities and of course we want to do England." No mention was made of the possibility of touring America, something he especially had no great desire to repeat. Jones had a different view, saying later: "I actually thought we should have gone back to the States to tour, but we never did." In fact, Grant was busy trying to set up the first North American tour since 1977. He didn't share Bonham's misgivings and hoped Plant, having agreed to the European dates, would be ready to tour more regularly.

A plan was hatched to play 19 dates, starting in Montreal on October 17. Queues formed at box offices, just like the old days. The tour was tentatively called Led Zeppelin – The 1980s Part One. Rehearsals began at Page's new home in Windsor but Bonham appeared depressed at the thought of another gruelling US tour. Now approaching middle age, he doubted his ability to play with the energy and stamina expected of Zeppelin's star drummer.

Due to start rehearsals at Page's house on September 24, instead he began a marathon binge, starting with vodka in his local pub at lunchtime. He eventually

ABOVE: By now John Bonham feared that age was taking its toll on his energy levels – the last thing he needed was another US tour.

LEFT: Happy memories – Robert Plant studies an album of snapshots.

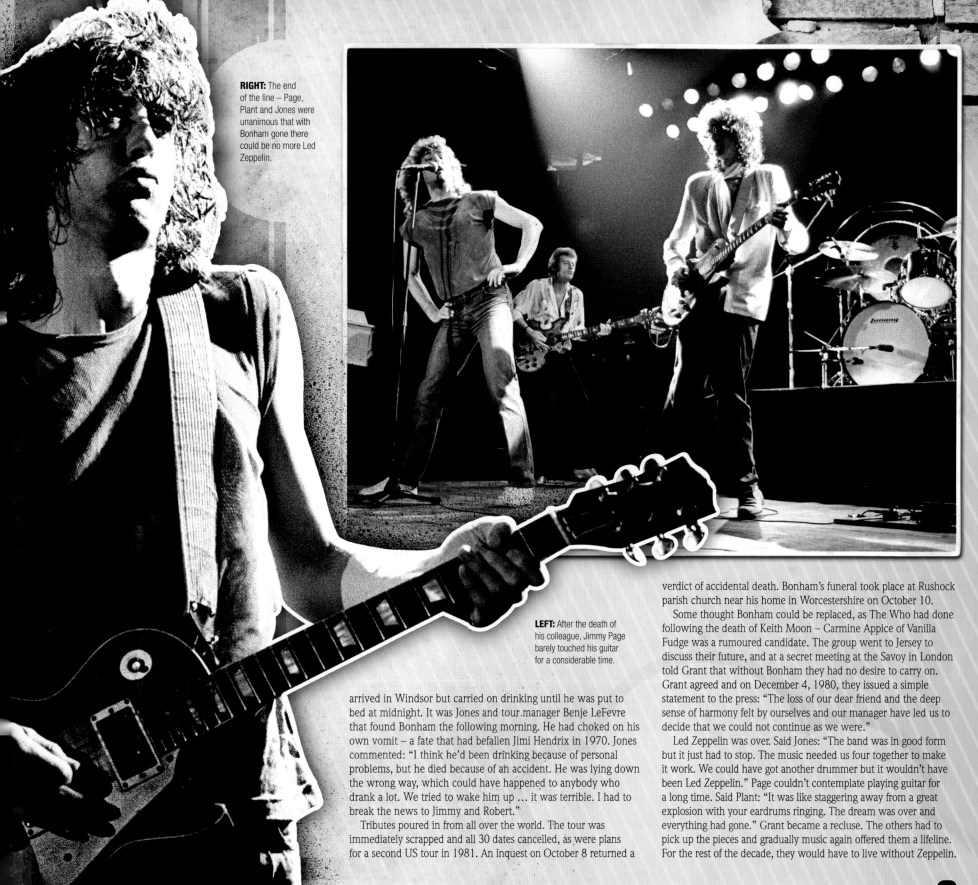

arrived in Windsor but carried on drinking until he was put to bed at midnight. It was Jones and tour manager Benje LeFevre that found Bonham the following morning. He had choked on his own vomit – a fate that had befallen Jimi Hendrix in 1970. Jones commented: "I think he'd been drinking because of personal problems, but he died because of an accident. He was lying down the wrong way, which could have happened to anybody who drank a lot. We tried to wake him up … it was terrible. I had to break the news to Jimmy and Robert."

Tributes poured in from all over the world. The tour was immediately scrapped and all 30 dates cancelled, as were plans for a second US tour in 1981. An inquest on October 8 returned a verdict of accidental death. Bonham's funeral took place at Rushock parish church near his home in Worcestershire on October 10.

Some thought Bonham could be replaced, as The Who had done following the death of Keith Moon – Carmine Appice of Vanilla Fudge was a rumoured candidate. The group went to Jersey to discuss their future, and at a secret meeting at the Savoy in London told Grant that without Bonham they had no desire to carry on. Grant agreed and on December 4, 1980, they issued a simple statement to the press: "The loss of our dear friend and the deep sense of harmony felt by ourselves and our manager have led us to decide that we could not continue as we were."

Led Zeppelin was over. Said Jones: "The band was in good form but it just had to stop. The music needed us four together to make it work. We could have got another drummer but it wouldn't have been Led Zeppelin." Page couldn't contemplate playing guitar for a long time. Said Plant: "It was like staggering away from a great explosion with your eardrums ringing. The dream was over and everything had gone." Grant became a recluse. The others had to pick up the pieces and gradually music again offered them a lifeline. For the rest of the decade, they would have to live without Zeppelin.

CODA

A poignant swansong emerged in the aftermath of Led Zeppelin's demise, but it took time for this 'song' – in the form of a final album – to be sung. In the turmoil of the early 1980s, as new musical fashions took hold, the very idea of the heavy rock group was deemed to be well past its sell-by date. But this ignored the sense of loss felt by fans worldwide, and the need for a line to be drawn under Zeppelin's recorded history. This came about with the release of their tenth and final album.

It was two years since Bonham's death. There had been no rush to pour out "tribute" albums, only a respectful silence and a long period of mourning. But feeling that Zeppelin deserved more than isolation and abandonment, Page set about compiling one last album as a tribute to John and to serve as as the group's memorial.

Zeppelin were contracted to produce another five albums for Atlantic on their Swan Song label. As it was impossible to produce new material, Page's solution was to go through the tapes stored at his home studio for unheard gems. He spent most of 1981 going through them all and making a final selection: eight tracks dating from 1969 to 1978. Plant and Jones were called in to help out with overdubs before they were ready for inclusion.

The appropriately named *Coda* was presented in a sombre grey and green gatefold sleeve that opened to reveal a montage of photographs showing Zeppelin on the road from the days of the 1970 Bath Festival to Knebworth in 1979.

The release was quite low-key, at least in the UK where pop groups such as Bucks Fizz gained more media attention: but the album again proved a huge seller, reaching Number 4 in the UK charts and Number 6 in America. Opener 'We're Gonna Groove' is a Ben E. King number played with all the zest of a confident young band making its way in a London studio in 1969. Plant's bluesy, echoing vocals are chased by Page's soulful guitar and while it's a somewhat chaotic production compared to later recordings, it sets a cheerful and optimistic mood for listeners delving into their own Zeppelin memories. Recorded at Morgan Studios on June 25, 1969, just before the Bath Festival and following a UK tour, it had been intended for *Led Zeppelin II*.

'Poor Tom' commences with a typically bluff and commanding drum rhythm, which Plant uses as a platform for his extemporizations. The feel is Delta blues and 'Poor Tom' sounds like a work song. Page's acoustic guitar chimes in the background of a recording made at Olympic Studios, Barnes, on June 5, 1970. The 'Poor Tom' of the story faces the noose, having shot his unfaithful wife. It might have been included on *Led Zeppelin III* but was supplanted by other Bron-Yr-Aur compositions.

'I Can't Quit You Baby' is Zeppelin's take on Willie Dixon's classic blues, recorded during a soundcheck at the Royal Albert Hall on January 9, 1970. As the concert was to be filmed, a Pye recording truck had been provided and the engineers fortuitously captured the band playing for themselves rather than an audience. The result was even better than the version on their debut

album. The empty hall gives great resonance to Plant's voice and Bonham's devastating drums; Zeppelin's dynamic range is fully explored as Jimmy's guitar alternately whispers and shouts and the mood leaps from frenzy to tantalizing delicacy. Jones' bass ensures the performance swings rather than rocks and Bonham's drumming ventures is like Elvin Jones meeting the blues.

'Walter's Walk' is a strident rock 'n' roll burn-up with layers of seemingly disconnected riffs stacking up over a pulsating heartbeat, Plant's near-hysterical delivery suiting the slightly manic tone. It was recorded using The Rolling Stones' mobile studio at Mick Jagger's home, Stargroves, in Berkshire on May 15, 1972, engineered by Eddie Kramer. Planned for *Houses of the Holy*, it made an exciting climax for Side 1 of *Coda*.

'Ozone Baby' is a rare pop performance, closer in spirit to Elvis Costello and Stiff Records than Willie Dixon. It's an interesting foray into new territory, although former session men Page and Jones could deliver this sort of performance at the tick of a studio clock. In fact the studio where this was conceived was Polar in Stockholm during the sessions for *In Through The Out Door*.

'Darlene' is another gem from the Polar album session in November 1978. It is a rock 'n' roll party track with Jones' boogie piano to the fore. There are pauses for piano and drum breaks and the jerky beat that launches the tune gives way to a swinging, saloon bar rave-up.

'Bonzo's Montreux' is a showcase for Bonham's skills, blending the bite of his acoustic drum kit with a special electronic treatment. Captured at Mountain Studios, Montreux, on September 12, 1976, it improved on the 'Moby Dick' solo featured on *Led Zeppelin II*. More creative and better recorded, it sounds as if Bonham is using a double bass drum, such is the speed and dexterity of his pedal work. Page called it the John Bonham Drum Orchestra and from his spot in the control room blended snare, tom-toms, timpani and timbales to build a wall of sound.

The album winds up with the raucous 'Wearing and Tearing', a breathless gallop that charges into the valley of rock with all cannons blazing. Sticking two fingers up to the punk rockers, it was to have been released as a single, under a different name, but unfortunately missed the deadline for the 1979 Knebworth show and didn't make it into *In Through The Out Door*.

Coda is a greater album than was thought at the time. Fans might have expected to find another 'Stairway To Heaven' or 'Kashmir' plucked from the archives: but it showed their music was always fresh, original and brilliantly performed, and that the band were always in competition with one very powerful rival – themselves.

"WE'RE THE BIGGEST BAND IN THE WORLD, SO WE'LL GO OUT THERE AND SHOW THEM WE STILL ARE!"

Peter Grant, on organising the now-legendary Knebworth appearance.

LEFT: (clockwise from top left) Jimmy Page, Robert Plant, John Bonham and John Paul Jones – four parts of a great equation.

JIMMY PAGE

Jimmy Page strutting the stage amid a blaze of laser beams, raising a violin bow and attacking the strings of his guitar while performing 'Dazed And Confused', is one of rock's iconic images: but behind the virtuoso showman lies a master musician.

Born James Patrick Page (January 9, 1944) in Heston, Middlesex, he grew up in a country house in Northampton belonging to a great-uncle. When he was eight, the family moved to Feltham, near London Airport. Jimmy had a happy childhood, took part in school sports and studied art. However, when his parents gave him a guitar for his 12th birthday his future was assured.

As airport noise grew worse the family moved again, to Epsom, Surrey, and Jimmy went to grammar school. The guitar had lain untouched for years, but one day he saw a boy singing skiffle and playing guitar on the playing-field and was impressed by the attention he was attracting. "I wondered how he did it and he showed me how to tune a guitar, and from then on I began going to guitar shops and watching other people play until people began watching me." Jimmy studied the book *Play In A Day* by Bert Weedon, but found musical theory difficult to master. What he really wanted to play was rock 'n' roll. He had begun to emulate his favourite records, copying the solos note for note.

Among his earliest influences was American session guitarist James Burton, but Jimmy also developed a fondness for vocal harmony groups, appreciating the way guitars were integrated into the production. This was matched by his discovery of the hardcore blues that lay at the heart of rock 'n' roll. Older friends would play him records by such artists as Sleepy John Estes and Arthur "Big Boy" Crudup, esoteric names unknown to most teenagers on either side of the Atlantic.

ABOVE: Dazed and Confused? On stage in 1974, Page plays his Les Paul guitar with a violin bow.

Another good place to hear the blues, jazz and soul was AFN, the American Forces radio network. At the same time he discovered folk music, and in particular the guitar work of Bert Jansch. "He was a real dream weaver and incredibly original." Page never had formal lessons, but claims: "I just picked it up. When I was at school I had my guitar confiscated every day. They handed it back to me each afternoon at four o'clock."

On leaving school he plunged straight into the business, joining Neil Christian and The Crusaders aged 15. To pay for his guitars and amplifiers, he delivered morning newspapers, but soon found himself earning good money; £20 a week. He spent most of it on better guitars, including a Gretsch Country Gentleman. Said Jeff Beck: "It looked huge on him, because he was such a shrimp. All you saw was a big guitar being thrown around by a kid who was as thin as a pipe-cleaner." Page, Beck and another up-and-coming guitarist, Eric Clapton, became firm friends in the so-called Surrey blues belt.

LEFT: Another iconic image – Page plays his trademark Gibson double-neck guitar.

The Crusaders played R&B, and the ever-improving guitarist began to make a name for himself. Said keyboard and bass player John Baldwin, later to become John Paul Jones: "I rated Jimmy Page for years. Even in 1962 I can remember people saying, 'You've got to listen to Neil Christian and The Crusaders. They've got an unbelievable young guitarist.'"

However, Jimmy grew tired of life on the road. He suffered from travel sickness and caught glandular fever. After collapsing from exhaustion, he left The Crusaders and played with blues harmonica man Cyril Davies at London's Marquee Club, but eventually left, not wishing to offend his former mentor Christian.

Aged 17, he decided to enrol at Sutton Art College, but while jamming at The Marquee was spotted by producer Mike Leander, who asked him if fancied some recording sessions. This meeting led to Page playing on hundreds of pop sessions in London between 1963 and 1966. Few session guys were capable of an authentic rock guitar sound, and Page found himself in demand. He played anonymously with big-name acts, notably The Kinks, Them and The Who, and worked alongside string and brass players, at the same time gaining an insight into studio technology. He was regarded as adaptable and reliable, and to his surprise found himself profiled in *The Sunday Times*' colour magazine.

Among the first groups Jimmy worked with was Carter-Lewis and The Southerners, later The Ivy League. He played on sessions with Lulu, Dave Berry, Donovan, P J Proby, Cliff Richard, Burt Bacharach, Tom Jones, Val Doonican and The Bachelors, began songwriting with singer Jackie DeShannon and worked with drummer Bobbie Graham on solo tracks.

Jimmy even cut a 1965 single, 'She Just Satisfies' (Fontana), on which he sang as well as playing guitar. Page worked with producer Mickie Most and arranged and produced tracks for Andrew Oldham's Immediate Records. In the end, however, he began to feel session work was a dead end. "There was no individuality involved. The arranger said: 'This is what you play', and that's what I played. I got fed up and it became a pain in the neck. When The Yardbirds came up, that was it."

In 1965 Page was invited to replace Clapton, who quit The Yardbirds in protest at their commerciality. Page didn't like the way the offer was presented and didn't fancy touring, so he recommended Beck. A year later, however, he saw them at an Oxford May Ball when singer Keith Relf freaked out on stage. Bassist Paul Samwell-Smith quit and Jimmy was asked to take over. He'd never played bass, and ultimately rhythm guitarist Chris Dreja took up this role while Page shared lead guitar duties with Beck. They began featuring "stereo sound" guitar duels, and the revitalized band went on a tour of America and also toured the UK supporting the Stones. However, after Beck's departure during a US tour in 1966, Page was left as sole lead guitarist. One number they began playing was 'Dazed And Confused', featuring Jimmy playing with a violin bow. The showman and leader was born.

WHAT HAPPENED NEXT

Led Zeppelin may have gone in 1980, but their music continued to inspire new generations. Metal developed at a phenomenal pace during the 1980s, and most acknowledged a debt to the masters: US grunge bands in the early 1990s cited Zeppelin as an important influence; copycats and tribute bands proliferated; Rolf Harris even took his version of 'Stairway To Heaven' into the charts in 1993. Once dismissed as "old hat", it seemed that everyone wanted them back.

Having agreed to go their separate ways the survivors faced uncertain futures. Plant wanted a solo career. Page, after Bonham's death, considered never playing again. Jones needed a new role in music. Grant chose retirement in a moated mansion – he would die in 1995, aged 60, of a heart attack. Plant described life in the aftermath: "I found myself standing on a street corner, clutching 12 years of my life, with a lump in my throat and tear in my eye, not knowing which way to go."

Jones quietly devoted himself to producing other bands, and would keep himself extremely busy over the next two decades combining production, film music and a low-key solo career.

Plant formed The Honeydrippers in 1981, and in July 1982 released solo album *Pictures At Eleven*, followed in 1983 by *The*

LEFT: Robert Plant and Alison Krauss, whose *Raising Sand* album received five Grammy awards.

ABOVE: There may be a few extra lines on the face, but Robert Plant shows that his vocal (and follicle) prowess is completely undiminished.

Principle Of Moments. That year Page returned to the stage for the ARMS charity shows at the Royal Albert Hall on September 20 and 21, in aid of research into multiple sclerosis, which had struck Ronnie Lane of The Faces. He jammed with Clapton and Beck and performed an instrumental version of 'Stairway To Heaven'. When the show went Stateside with guest singer Paul Rodgers, he and Page formed a new group, The Firm. He also cut an album with old friend Roy Harper, *Whatever Happened To Jugula?*, released in March 1985. The Firm's debut album in February 1985 coincided with a 32-date US tour. In April they played at Madison Square Garden and in May at Wembley Arena, Page delighting audiences by once more wielding his violin bow – this time on a number called 'The Chase'.

Plant also toured the US with his band to support third album *Shaken 'n' Stirred*. Then on July 13, 1985, all three reunited for Live Aid at the JFK Stadium, Philadelphia. Backed by drummers Tony Thompson and Phil Collins, who flew in on Concorde, they played 'Rock And Roll', 'Stairway To Heaven' and 'Whole Lotta Love'. This fuelled rumours of a full-scale reunion and in January 1986 secret rehearsals took place with Thompson in England until Plant decided to pull out. Another get-together came on May 14, 1988, at an Atlantic Records 40th Birthday concert at Madison Square Garden, this time with Bonham's son, Jason, on drums.

The Firm released one more album, *Mean Business*, before Page broke up the band. A solo debut, *Outrider*, was released in June 1988 and he toured with a new band including singer John Miles and Jason Bonham. Plant put out two more solo albums, *Now And Zen* in 1988 and *Manic Nirvana* in 1990, with a

European tour in May. On June 30 he and Page performed three Zeppelin songs at the *Silver Clef* concert at Knebworth.

On September 7, 1990, a 54-track boxed set, *Led Zeppelin*, digitally remastered in New York by Page and George Marino, was released on six albums, four cassettes and four CDs. A second boxed set came in 1993.

Page teamed up with Whitesnake's David Coverdale for *Coverdale Page*, released in March 1993, and toured Japan. Plant released *Fate Of Nations* and completed another US tour, commenting: "I love what we did in Led Zeppelin. Some of it was superb. I also remember some of the conditions it was created in, some of it not so good. But none of that matters because Led Zeppelin is a timepiece. You have to move on." However, he and Page did collaborate again; 1994 saw the release of CD and video *No Quarter: Unledded*, followed by a world tour.

In April 1998 came a second Page–Plant studio album, *Walking Into Clarksdale*, recorded at Abbey Road; the single 'Most High' won a Grammy. They also played at an Amnesty International concert in Paris in December, performing 'Gallows Pole', 'Rock And Roll' and 'Babe I'm Gonna Leave You'. In November 1999 *Early Days: The Best of Led Zeppelin Volume One* was released, followed a year later by *Volume Two, Latter Days*.

On December 14, 2006, Atlantic's founder Ahmet Ertegun died aged 83. This would trigger the reunion the fans had been awaiting – a concert in his memory. Twenty-five million people applied for twenty thousand tickets in an online ballot. On December 10, 2007, Page, Plant, Jones and Jason Bonham took the stage at the O2 Arena in London for what many hoped would be the beginning of a new era. The concert was a critical success but Plant quickly moved to quash rumours of any permanent reunion. He had only just achieved his greatest personal success with the million-selling, Grammy-winning *Raising Sand*, recorded with bluegrass singer Alison Krauss.

The former rock rebels were now establishment figures. Page was made an OBE in 2005 for charity work in Brazil and represented the UK at the Olympic closing ceremony in Beijing in August 2008, playing 'Whole Lotta Love'. In July 2009 Plant became a CBE. Regarding yet more reunion rumours, his parting comment was brief: "I wish Jimmy Page, John Paul Jones and Jason Bonham nothing but success with any future projects."

RIGHT: Jimmy Page once again takes to the stage with one of his mighty arsenal of Gibson Les Pauls.

BELOW: A wristband from Led Zeppelin's hugely successful reunion concert, a tribute to Ahmet Ertegun, founder of Atlantic Records.

ABOVE: In front of 20,000 people at the O2 Arena, London.

LEFT: John Paul Jones on stage with "supergroup" Them Crooked Vultures.

RIGHT: The new Zeppelin keep it in the family with Jason Bonham taking over the drum stool from his father.

ROCKOGRAPHY

LED ZEPPELIN ALBUMS

1969   *Led Zeppelin* (Atlantic)
       Led Zeppelin II (Atlantic)
1970   *Led Zeppelin III* (Atlantic)
1971   *Four Symbols* (Atlantic)
1973   *Houses Of The Holy* (Atlantic)
1975   *Physical Graffiti* (Swan Song)
1976   *Presence* (Swan Song)
       The Song Remains The Same (Swan Song)
1979   *In Through The Out Door* (Swan Song)
1982   *Coda* (Swan Song)
1997   *BBC Sessions* (Atlantic)
2003   *How The West Was Won* (Atlantic)

LED ZEPPELIN COMPILATION ALBUMS

1990   *Led Zeppelin* (Atlantic)
       Led Zeppelin Remasters (Atlantic)
1993   *Led Zeppelin Boxed Set 2* (Atlantic)
       The Complete Studio Recordings (Atlantic)
1999   *Early Days: Best Of Led Zeppelin Volume One* (Atlantic)
2000   *Latter Days: Best Of Led Zeppelin Volume Two* (Atlantic)
2002   *Early Days And Latter Days* (Atlantic)
2007   *Mothership* (Atlantic)
2008   *Definitive Collection* (Atlantic/Rhino)

LED ZEPPELIN SINGLES

1969   'Good Times Bad Times'
       'Whole Lotta Love'
1970   'Living Loving Maid (She's Just a Woman)'
       'Immigrant Song'
1971   'Black Dog'
1972   'Rock And Roll'
1973   'Over the Hills and Far Away'
       'D'yer Mak'er'
       'The Ocean'
1975   'Trampled Underfoot'

1976   'Candy Store Rock'
1979   'Fool In The Rain'
1982   'Darlene'
       'Ozone Baby'
       'Poor Tom'
1990   'Travelling Riverside Blues'
1993   'Baby Come On Home'
1997   'Whole Lotta Love'
       'The Girl I Love She Got Long Black Wavy Hair'
2007   'Whole Lotta Love'
       'Immigrant Song'
       'Black Dog'
       'Stairway to Heaven'
       'Kashmir'
       'Ramble On'

Changes in UK chart regulations in 2005 meant that it became possible for a song to get into the charts on downloads alone. All of the 2007 'singles' listed above reached the UK singles charts in this way, *not* because they were 'released' by the record label.

JOHN PAUL JONES ALBUMS

1985   *Scream For Help Soundtrack* (Atlantic)
1994   *The Sporting Life* (with Diamanda Galás) (Mute)
1999   *Zooma* (DGM)
2001   *The Thunderthief* (DGM)
2009   *Them Crooked Vultures* (Columbia/Interscope)
2011   *You Can't Teach An Old Dog New Tricks* (with Seasick Steve)
2013   *Hubcap Music* (with Seasick Steve)

Them Crooked Vultures is a contemporary "super group" made up of John Paul Jones, Josh Homme from Queens Of The Stone Age and Dave Grohl of Nirvana/Foo Fighters.

JIMMY PAGE SOLO ALBUMS

1982   *Death WIsh II Soundtrack* (Swan Song)
1984   *The Honeydrippers: Volume One* (with Jimmy Page) (Es Paranza)
1985   *Whatever Happened to Jugula?* (with Roy Harper) (Beggars Banquet)
1985   *The Firm* (with The Firm) (Atlantic)
1986   *Mean Business* (with The Firm) (Atlantic)
1986   *Strange Land* (with Box of Frogs) (Renaissance)
1988   *Outrider* (Geffen)
1993   *Coverdale-Page* (Geffen/EMI)
1994   *No Quarter* (with Robert Plant) (Atlantic/Fontana)
1998   *Walking into Clarksdale* (with Robert Plant) (Atlantic/Mercury)
2000   *Live at the Greek* (Jimmy Page and The Black Crowes) (Musicmaker)
2012   *Luicfier Rising and Other Sound Tracks*

ROBERT PLANT ALBUMS

1982   *Pictures At Eleven* (Swan Song)
1983   *The Principle Of Moments* (Es Paranza)
1984   *The Honeydrippers: Volume One* (with Jimmy Page) (Es Paranza)
1985   *Shaken 'n' Stirred* (Es Paranza)
1988   *Now And Zen* (Es Paranza)
1990   *Manic Nirvana* (Es Paranza)
1993   *Fate Of Nations* (Es Paranza)
1994   *No Quarter* (with Jimmy Page) (Atlantic/Fontana)
1998   *Walking Into Clarksdale* (with Jimmy Page) (Atlantic)
2002   *Dreamland* (Mercury)
2005   *Mighty ReArranger* (Sanctuary)
2007   *Raising Sand* (with Alison Krauss)
2010   *Band of Joy* (Decca/Rounder)

PICTURE CREDITS

The publishers would like to thank the following sources for their kind permission to reproduce the photographs in this book.

Key: t = top, b = bottom, l = left, r = right and c = centre

Corbis: /Alesandra Benedetti: 90r

Rudi Daugsch: 9bc

Getty Images: 6-7, 8 (x4), 11 (x4), 20r, 33l, 65r, 85r, 91br; / Buzzfoto/FilmMagic: 81tr; /Redferns: 9br, 12l, 12r, 13tr, 13bc, 14, 15bl, 21r, 33br, 36-37, 40, 41l, 41r, 42l, 42r, 43r, 48, 49r, 53tr, 59l, 62r, 63r, 68, 72r, 80, 81br, 82l, 83l, 83r, 85l, 88l, 89r, 95; /Michael Ochs Archive: 24-25bc, 29br, 32bl, 34bc, 43l, 46cr, 54l, 69, 70, 72l, 73b, 74-75, 86-87; /Time & Life Pictures: 15tr, 16-17, 23tl, 23tr, 56-57, 77l, 79l, 81bl; / Wireimage: 55tr, 77r, 91c

© Bob Gruen: 34r, 52l, 53r, 59br, 66-67

The Kobal Collection: /Starmavale/Swan Song: 65l

Bob Masse: 9bl, 33tr

Mirrorpix: 15br

Ikumi Numata: 44l, 44-45, 49br

Press Association Images: /AP Photo: 90bl; /Suzan: 91tr

Private Collection: 9tr, 18, 22, 28, 58, 84, 91b

Photoshot: /Michael Putland/Retna: 19, 26-27, 46br, 52r, 62l, 64r, 76bl; /Peter Mazel/Sunshine/Retna: 53c; /Retna Pictures: 89bc; /Sunshine/Retna: 76r; /Ronald van Caem/Tolca/ Sunshine/Retna: 78-79b; /Chris Walter/Photofeatures/Retna: 24bl, 31, 64bl

Rex Features: /Blake-Ezra Cole: 91cl; /James Fortune: 47t, 47b, 49l, 63l; /Globe Photos Inc.: 4; /Ilpo Musto: 20l, 35, 82r, 88r; /Ray Stevenson: 29tl, 72c; /Richard Young: 21l

Rob Roth/Paul Grushkin: 30l, 38tr, 60-61, 71tl, 71r, 78bl, 96

Tracks: 2, 10, 25t, 30tr, 30br, 32r, 38l, 39, 50tl, 50r, 51, 71bl

Urbanimage.tv: 54r, 55l, 55br, 93; /Adrian Boot: 79c

Frank White Photo Agency: /Ron Aki: 73l

Every effort has been made to acknowledge correctly and contact the source and/or copyright holder of each picture and Carlton Books Limited apologises for any unintentional errors or omissions, which will be corrected in future editions of this book.

"THERE IS NOTHING INHERENT MUSICALLY IN LED ZEPPELIN TO HARM OR DESTROY."

Robert Plant, 1970.

遂に待望のときが来た！最大のロック・グループ《レッド・ツェッペリン》狂熱のライブが始まる！

レッド・ツェッペリン

狂熱のライブ

IN CONCERT AND BEYOND

LED·ZEPPELIN

THE·SONG·REMAINS·THE·SAME